Grat Goldmine

Dig Deep, Feel Great(Ful)

By
Sarit Gafan

Copyright © 2024 by Sarit Gafan

The author has asserted her right to be identified as the author of this work in accordance with the Copyright, Design and Patents Act 1988. The contents of this book may not be reproduced in any form without written permission of the author, except for short extracts, quotations or review.

Contents

Universal Gratitude	5
Foreword	11
Chapter 1: Reader Meet Gratitude	21
Chapter 2: Gratitude for Wellbeing	35
Chapter 3: Gratitude for Spiritual Journey	53
Chapter 4: Gratitude for Cultivating Positive Experiences	65
Chapter 5: Your Floor Could Be Someone's Ceiling	75
Chapter 6: Your Journey with Gratitude	89
Chapter 7: My Journey with Gratitude - 14 Day Challenge Invitation	99
Chapter 8: Heartful Conclusions	149
Pool of Practices	153
References	162

To all beings stuck on the bottom level of the pyramid of needs, may you receive all the help and resources you need.

May you receive the healing you need to reach your self-actualisation and find your unique purpose.

May we all awaken to who we are, what we have and what we are here to do for the Highest Good of this planet and all her inhabitants.

Acknowledgements
Universal Gratitude

To the true author of this book, the Divine Universal Source, and to Mother Earth and all the guides and higher energies supporting me - I wholeheartedly and wholesouledly thank you. Thank you for your divine connection, for helping me find my purpose, and for all the light you pour into me every day in order to fulfil it. Thank you for showing what the best kind of attention I can give is - love. Thank you Mother Earth for all the blessings, beauty and abundance you provide every day. Thank you for offering me a place to be truly myself and welcoming me to just be without asking anything of me. Thank you for providing me with food and water that works in harmony with my whole being and helps me to hear my inner voice and flow onward on my soul's journey.

Firstly, I wish to thank my parents for bringing me into this world. Thank you Mum and Dad for doing your very best to bring me up with the principles that have shaped me and for giving me the very best life you possibly could, especially during the difficult times in my life. Thank you.

To my inspiring sister Shelli, from one PG to another, thank you for always reminding me to believe in myself.

To my beloved partner Jerome, thank you for accepting my weird, wild and wonderful ways. Thank you for your enduring support and for lovingly pushing me to get my stuff out there.

To my dear friend Geri, 'mo anam cara', my soul friend. Thank you for being the sounding board for all my musings, writing and learning. No words can truly express the love I have felt from you since we became friends, but as a writer I would like to try. No matter what life brings, when we connect I feel as though I am walking this life as if through a divine field of light with you by my side, totally seen, totally loved, totally accepted and at peace. Walking with you is like walking in nature. This gift you have given me is priceless. It has helped me be me, the true me that I wish for everyone to be able to be, and because of your unfaltering support I have put so much more of myself out into the world. Thank you for your love, your patience, your music and of course, your tea! I can only hope to be of the same support to you as you are to me. Thank you for helping me bring The Gratitude Song to life - without you it would probably still be just a bunch of notes! Thank you dear friend, with all my heart and soul.

Thank you to all my friends and loved ones for encouraging me on my journey and for never getting tired of hearing "It's nearly finished!".

Deepest Gratitude to my dear friend Al Cropley for all your patience and kindness in helping me set up my company. You're a legend!

Greatest Gratitude to my wonderful friend Lola Askarova for her kind, encouraging, wise and amazingly balanced insight on my journey into authentic business.

Thank you to the members of my focus group, who took the time to read my final draft and share their thoughts and perspectives with kind candour. Thank you to the wonderful friends who took the time to read parts of my manuscript, including Geri O'Regan and Michael Capocci.

To my friend and past client SD and your cats R and M, thank you for giving me the opportunity to see into your world and for the privilege of working with you for a while. I have learnt so much from our time together and I hope and pray that what I share with the world will somehow come back to you in the form of the greatest quality of life.

I am deeply grateful to Victoria Johnson, Co-Founder and Director of the Museum of Happiness, and Shamash Alidina, Author of Mindfulness for Dummies, for giving me the opportunity to share some of what I've learned about Gratitude through my work with the Museum. Thank you for giving me faith that what I have to share is of value to the world. Thank you both for believing in me, encouraging me and supporting my work. You truly live your values and are certainly being the change that you and I wish to see in the world!

I express my deepest Gratitude and admiration to Andrew Faris, Founder and CEO of Rhythms of Life homelessness charity, for teaching me what unconditional service can look like and for trusting me to share a little of his story.

I extend my greatest Gratitude to Masa Fredrick and the Together We Love Ministry community for everything you have taught, and are still teaching me, and for allowing me to share some of your story.

Greatest Gratitude to the charity 2econd Chance, who gifted me the laptop and equipment I needed to be able to write this book and run my business when I was not able to replace mine, and to Inclusion Barnet who arranged this for me.

Deep Gratitude bow to Steve Nobel and his team for all the incredible work and resources you put out into the world to support people like me who just want to bring more love into the world.

I thank with all my heart and soul all the family of Lightworkers, Healers, Starseeds, Earth Angels and all my fellow Tao Hands Practitioners working every day to pour as much light and love as they can into this world under the extraordinary and life challenging circumstances and conditions of this current time. Thank you for holding space here to make this world a better place, spread unity consciousness and help heal our beautiful Earth. Thank you for your unconditional service. Thank you for getting up every day to do it all again.

A heartfelt thank you to Illa and Jeetu Khagram, Certified Master Teachers of the Tao Academy™, for all your love, healing, guidance and support on my journey.

I am so grateful to Dr and Master Zhi Gang Sha for everything I have learnt from you and all the healing and transformation that has arisen in me since I became a Tao Hands Practitioner. Thank you for bringing so much light and so many gifts into this world. Thank you for spreading so much 'positive information' and showing people how to use it.

With my hand on my heart, I thank all the brilliant practitioners who have each helped me become a little more myself, supporting me at one time or another with their unique services, including: Cristina Lorefice, T C Kelly, Deborah Laurence, Donna Katae, Lori Frischkorn, Diana Radneva, Jessica Ann, Mikhail of the Global Circle of Sovereign Beings, my Phil Parker Lightning Process® (LP) instructor and so many others who supported me on my spiritual and self-development journey unconditionally.

Thank you to all the amazing people and organisations who have supported me and the energies that synergised to enable me to have the time and space to allow this book to flow through me, the freedom to write and express my authentic self, and the courage, confidence and self-belief to actually hit the publish button. I bow to you in Gratitude.

I am grateful for all the experiences that have led me to publish this book.

I am deeply grateful to Ali of @ebook_experts and his team on Fiverr for their patience, professionalism and compassion in helping me on my fledgling journey into the world of EBook publishing.

I thank with all my heart, Raisha Islam of @pindesign_town on Fiverr, for her open-heartedness and artistry in creating my beautiful book cover.

Finally, I wouldn't be completely authentic if I didn't break with convention (a little more!). There are many other souls whom I have not mentioned by name, but to whom I am truly grateful simply for loving me. Thank you. Through that love, I have become more at ease in this world. One of these souls is me. Thank you Sarit for never giving up. I love you.

Foreword

So much has been said and written about Gratitude and the benefits of practising it, but it has a very special place in my heart. It took me by the hand while I was just learning to grow into my own skin and accept that life was always going to feel difficult because I thought that the world was telling me I wasn't good enough and didn't belong here. It showed me that there is so much goodness within me and around me. That helped me defy and reverse the negative programming and conditioning that had been telling me that there is much to fear and that listening to your heart is a foolish and frivolous way to live. Above all, it is helping me to open my heart to the sheer wonders of this life more and more, so I can live a happier, healthier one, and I want that for you too!

I may not be writing this book from my pearl pink yacht off the coast of some glamorous island, but I am writing it from my heart - wearing my heart on my book sleeve if you like. My success story goes deeper than fame or fortune. I have learnt to stop trying to fit in and to love, accept and believe in myself despite feeling completely out of place in this world, enough to write a book!

The term 'Gratitude Goldmine' flew into my consciousness when I had started teaching Gratitude practice through my work with the Museum of Happiness. I was researching amazing facts about the body and the things around us that make life easy for us and meet our basic needs without us blinking. For example, I discovered that there are around 2 million working parts in each eye, and if we are fortunate enough to wake up with good vision, that is because around 2 million miracles happened.

To me, it felt like I had struck gold.

It felt like I had become aware of a secret world of wonders that was just beneath the surface and needed only a little attention to be blessed by it. We each have our own Gratitude Goldmine, our own world of wonders that, if we take the time to explore it and discover its gifts, can bring us a sense of peace that so much is going right for us all the time and a shield of resilience.

But you have to be willing to dig!

Digging into your Gratitude Goldmine involves purposeful, kind, mindful, curious and positive thinking about what is going right for you in any given moment.

Developing the skills to dig into my own Gratitude Goldmine has been a challenging, enlightening and uplifting journey so far. Meandering roads of learning that led me to the unique and wonderful ways I now enjoy practising it.

It takes patience, commitment and a willingness to be flexible and even playful, which is why I have written this book - to help you on your own journey of learning how to dig deep and explore for yourself how much is going right for you all the time. 'Digging deep' means being prepared to invest time, headspace and heartspace in finding the things you can be grateful for in your daily life - along with personalised ways to make this practice meaningful and beneficial for you and your life.

After 15 years of depression, Gratitude helped me transform my life, providing me with an outlook that not only cushions the bumps in the road but facilitates flow. Life feels lighter and more fun, and I find that I am able to flow more easily (and more gracefully!) through the ups and downs of life. I have also felt closer to Mother Earth and more deeply connected to the highest energy I call the Divine Source.

Gratitude has become embedded in my thinking so that I can often apply it **in the moment**, rather than only in retrospect, which has helped me reconnect with the happy, playful and peaceful person I truly am.

How did Gratitude become a part of my mental decor? I'll cover that in detail later, but it wasn't an overnight job. Through a series of magical moments over the years, I have found my way to deeper learnings, creative practices and mindful thought prompts.

It began when I finally broke out of the depression. The relief I felt at being able to see myself as the kind, positive, worthy and functioning person that I truly am, was the stimulus that triggered the initial deep sense of Gratitude. I realise now that it wasn't that depression had changed me, reduced my value or made me a lesser person, it was simply a weighted veil that had kept my light hidden, but hidden from me, more than others. I remember in the depths of this experience, during my first attempt at university, a fellow student told me how positive I was, but the depression intercepted my ability to believe it.

By writing this book, I have discovered that the actual practising of Gratitude came into my life at a time when I took a leap of faith to do some soul searching. I left full time paid work and have as yet never returned to it, honouring my soul's journey of learning, healing and starting a mental wellbeing company to share what I have learned. This has meant that I have been living on a part time income for several years, with the support of my incredible partner and my beloved parents and other loved ones, without whom I would not have had the freedom and privilege to be able to take this journey. The last 7 years have been a journey of awakening for me, learning to appreciate the privileges and challenges of life on a slimline income. This journey is still unfolding to my surprise and delight, with this most recent of epiphanies:

The Universe responded to my leap of faith by offering me the companion of Gratitude on my journey.

I have still not been fully able to embrace it, because (like every human) I am a world, and I have been responding to conflicts within my world and healing as much as I can. However, Gratitude practice has played a significant role in that healing too. At the beginning of my journey, Gratitude arose in me naturally, when things were going well and there were many things that came easily to me. I was unaware then that if we became best friends it would be there for me at the times I needed it most, like a loyal team mate. In order for that relationship to develop, I realised that I need to practise it all the time, even when things are going well!

I see Gratitude as part of a wellbeing focused lifestyle that can bring more peace and joy, as well as an energy that can uplift this world. I've written this book to share that ideology because I have a deep desire to help people who find life's ups and downs tough to handle and to cultivate a kinder, happier, more peaceful and loving world.

I feel called to share at this juncture, some information that may serve readers in approaching this book in their own ways from the outset. On my journey of self-discovery, I have learned much about my brain and energy type. I do not wish to exclude anyone from receiving the benefits of my learning so please note the following. In the modality of Human Design, I am a Reflector energy type. We make up only 1.5% of the population and my interpretation of our main purpose is to reflect and amplify energy to show what needs positive attention. As Reflectors are experiencing the energy of the people and environments around us all the time, our energy levels can be highly inconsistent. This means different things to different Reflectors, but I have found that while there are practices that have become part of my life's furniture, I tend to dip into most practices for a while, or some kind of 'season', and then move on. So the practices I share are not all ones that I practise regularly. I feel that part of my purpose in writing this book is to provide new and creative ideas for people to try out for themselves, whether I practise them consistently or not. I have also learned that I have traits of a mind consistent with an

ADHD brain type. With all of the above in mind, I have done my best to be true to my role of reflecting what needs more positive attention in this area of work. Please remember that you too are a world, and your experiences and rhythms may be completely different. I invite you to notice how you learn throughout this book, with an open mind and kindness to yourself. The keys to developing self-kindness are, I believe, learning not to judge yourself and remembering that you are always consciously doing your best. I am passionate about personalised learning and believe with all my heart in following your own unique ways of learning - I hope that my approach to the learning in this book will support that.

I have found that Gratitude, when applied in my own way and at the right times for me, is a great tool for:

- Wellbeing
- Spiritual Journey
- Cultivating Positive Experiences.

I invite you to read with an open heart and an open mind and find your own special and nourishing ways with it, so I have reserved a whole chapter for you at the end to dig deep and explore your own Gratitude Goldmine! I'd like as much as possible for us to take this journey together, not just you reading about mine, but you exploring yours, so I've added an invitation for Reader Reflections with space to jot your musings and any magical epiphanies that might occur to you at the end of the chapters.

My intention for this book is to show how my journey with Gratitude has nourished me, so that you can explore its benefits for your own life and maybe even experience the ripple effect! I also believe that the world can be a better place simply by the energy we fill ourselves with, and the energy we send out into it. I have enjoyed first-hand experience of improved experiences and interactions simply by appreciating people's situations and efforts, even if it is their job to provide a service.

How to get the best out of this book

This book has been designed to offer theory along with reflections and practices to embed the learning, and I invite you to find your own way through the content. For example, if you prefer to read it all the way through and then try the practices, then do that. Go at a pace that feels nourishing and right for you.

The Kindful Reader Reflections act as a kind and wise learning buddy, to invite you to apply my learning to your own experiences. Kindfulness is simply the non-judgemental observation inherent in mindfulness practice, accompanied by kindness, and I have experienced firsthand what mindfulness expert Shamash Alidina states, that "it reminds you to be forgiving and friendly as you practise" (Alidina, S, 2015). Please take good care of yourself when doing them, especially if you feel triggered by something, and make sure that you get any support you need.

There is a 14 day challenge in Chapter 7 - Your Journey With Gratitude. This is an invitation to welcome Gratitude as your companion for 14 days, reading one of the vignettes at a time, with the option of reflecting on and practising Gratitude. The first seven days of the challenge are accompanied by guided reflections and practises, with the last seven days being left open for your own. If you prefer a simpler version, you could just commit to practising Gratitude in your own ways for 5 minutes a day, for 14 days or as long as feels right. Either way, I invite you to reflect and record your practice to see how it affects your energy, and more specifically, your wellbeing, spiritual journey and positive experiences, or in any areas of your life!

With wellbeing in mind, it's important to notice how you're feeling when you read the book, especially when you engage with the practices. I invite you to check in with yourself and see if you're in the right space to do so. For example, if you're feeling a little low, it could be that the reading and practices will nudge you up to a better place (as they have done for me!). However, if you're feeling really low, please be kind to yourself: if it feels right and kind to push yourself to read and practice, then do that, but if it feels like you're forcing yourself, or judging yourself for not trying, then I invite you to just focus on taking great care of yourself. You can also try out my Self-Care Check In, a short practice to help you tune in to how you're feeling, without judgement.

When it comes to your learning from this book and engaging with its practices, please don't worry about what 'the right way' is but instead find out what 'your way' is. The only suggestion I would like to offer, if your goal is to create a Gratitude habit of your own, is to spend some time with your new companion at least once a day during the challenge - this will begin to develop your relationship!

I invite you to see what wants to follow you out of the book – what speaks to you or is highlighted for you in your own life. If it feels good and safe, follow it, go with it and see where it takes you, see what nourishing experiences it might lead you to.

DISCLAIMER: I want all my readers to be safe, well and healthy. Please make sure that you prioritise health and safety, yours and others', when reading, learning and practising from this book. Please also note that the intention here is to offer knowledge and tools for positive effect in your life, and as such is not medical advice nor should it replace any medical treatment or professional help you are receiving.

Kindful Reader Reflections

What does Gratitude mean to you now, as you begin on this journey of exploration?

How does your current relationship with Gratitude look and feel? Record this in any way you feel called to.

Chapter 1

Reader Meet Gratitude

Hello there! My name is Gratitude and I've got a lot of great energy to share. I may be as old as time, but I'm still growing and evolving every day. People are connecting with me in new, creative and heart-expanding ways every day, and in doing that they're spreading a really positive message throughout the world, from their lives outwards. So how about it? Want to hang out for a while?

The first thing you need to know about me is that I give out a **really** good energy vibration: kindness, peace, mindfulness, abundance, love, enjoyment, contentment and more. Do you want more of that in your life? I'm handing over to Sarit, she and I are old friends and she's got a really good grasp on what I want to bring to the world, 'coz I've been whispering in her ear for quite some time.

Sarit: Ah wow, thank you Gratitude! Who could have known that one day I'd be saying "Thank You" to Gratitude itself?

As I mentioned at the start, the 3 key areas that have been positively impacted by embedding Gratitude into my mindset and my daily life are:

- Wellbeing
- Spiritual Journey
- Cultivating Positive Experiences.

In writing this book, I have discovered that all three benefits are beautifully interlinked and that the underlying theory I have come to understand about Gratitude has deepened my practice and enhanced my life in the following ways:

Wellbeing

There are many studies showing the health benefits of Gratitude practice. The Greater Good Science Center at the University of California is a hub of scientific Gratitude studies and the academic home of leading Gratitude expert, Robert Emmons. They include Gratitude as one of their keys to wellbeing, and in Chapter 2, I will share my own real life examples of this.

In general, the theory and practice of Gratitude have provided me with a sense of positive grounding in a world that could have easily continued to eat me up and spit me out, just as it did at the age of 15 when I fell into a 15 year journey into depression. It has supported me in being myself more, as I LOVE being positive and freely and sincerely appreciating things and people as much as I possibly can!

I used to hate the world. I didn't feel like I belonged. So when the depression kicked in, it was all too easy to feel like it was hating me back. I felt like I was being eaten alive by the judgements of society, even though I wasn't aware that that's what I was feeling, I just felt deeply miserable but I didn't understand why. The world has changed considerably since I was in my teens, but I have identified a number of factors that I believe contribute to the collective perspective I feel from so many people that life is hard.

We live in a largely fast-paced, material and achievement oriented society, where, until recently, slowing down and taking care of ourselves has not been valued, more seen as weak, frowned upon and possibly even an excuse to shirk. This means that most people are constantly pushing or forcing themselves to do more and have more. We are also being continuously programmed (by people who want us to spend our money on their products or provide them with our personal data) to think that we need new 'things and stuff' all the time in order to live a better life or to be healthier, happier or a better version of ourselves. Of course, this can be true if something genuinely does that in the best way for you, but the mass selling that goes on is constantly giving us the message that we need more more and more of things that are not necessarily designed with our uniqueness in mind.

Society seems to have decided upon very specific and limited visions of what happiness, beauty, health and success look like, and as a result, many of us feel unhappy, unattractive, unhealthy and unsuccessful!

In addition to this, our primaeval survival-oriented wiring, the Negativity Bias, means that our brains are naturally programmed to look for threats and respond to them as **life or death** situations. This is our 'Fight or Flight' response, which activates when we feel threatened by a range of stressful situations (from relationship difficulties and financial strain to actual life-threatening situations).

Disproportionate weight has been given to the realm of the mind over the heart and the value of emotions is generally seen as lower or an inconvenience, and as for the soul, well, in my opinion, let's just say we still have a lot of waking up to do about that!

We are constantly being bombarded by information in our homes, through our devices, when we travel, in fact wherever we go; multiple, often sales-focused streams of it coming from advertising, media and more, carrying fear based narratives or telling us that we are not good enough as we are. Furthermore, our mobile phones are no longer simply used for making calls - they are now portable offices, which makes it much harder to switch off from work. All this makes it more difficult to achieve the external and internal peace and quiet we need to hear our own truth, our inner voice, and to fully enjoy our human experiences in our own way and at our own pace.

I believe that these factors contribute to our inability to appreciate what's going right in our lives more, and it is in pondering this that I recalled a psychological model from my earliest days at university.

Abraham Maslow created the Hierarchy of Needs to reflect what motivates humans (Maslow, A, 1943).

The pyramid of the Hierarchy of Needs is a visual representation of Maslow's theory. For those unable to see colour or viewing in grayscale, please note that each level of the pyramid is in a different colour, starting at the bottom with red, followed by orange, yellow, green and finally blue at the top.

Maslow's hierarchy of needs

Source: www.simplypsychology.org with kind permission from Saul McLeod PhD

The theory states that only when your basic needs, in other words your physiological and safety needs, are met, can you truly fulfil your higher ones of Love, Belonging, Esteem and Self-Actualisation, realising your full potential.

Maslow created the Hierarchy of Needs to show what motivates human behaviour, but I feel that if approached with kind mindfulness, it can serve as a reality check, a tool to help us stay grounded in turbulent times and clearly see which of the most important things are going right for us, or even sustaining us all the time - the things we may be taking for granted.

For me, Gratitude practice and the deeper theory I have explored around it, is part of a wider wellbeing mindset and lifestyle I have developed for myself. It has helped me maintain a positive outlook, counteracting the Negativity Bias and its effect on society, enabling me to live life as I wish to,

In a Positivity Bias!

At the age of 15, I had no strategies to deal with all the difficult emotions I experienced from living in this world, but at 47 I am incredibly grateful to have found, developed and embedded the right ones for me. My work with Gratitude, along with all the great work being done around the world, feels like it is helping to heal the world, from the inside of me, outwards.

As for my mental wellbeing, embedding Gratitude practice into my way of thinking has supported it several ways. Chapter 2 describes these in detail, but effectively, practising Gratitude has helped me to train my brain to think and feel more positively about situations, challenges and the world, and my belonging in it. It has helped me deal with and bounce back from many of life's ups and downs and forms part of my wellbeing toolkit and cultivated positive new emotions and experiences.

While the above benefits have most noticeably and measurably improved my mental wellbeing, I have also experienced some of the physical benefits mentioned in scientific studies. These are less concrete and harder to connect directly to my practice of Gratitude, but I can tell you that since making it a part of my lifestyle, I feel that my physical health is significantly more robust and resilient and I have a much happier relationship with my body.

Spiritual Journey

Another facet to my journey with Gratitude has been embracing it as an anchor for feeling supported and taken care of by this good, kind energy that I feel is the Divine Source. Believing that this Universe and the energy of lovingkindness that flows through it has helped me navigate this life with hope, positivity and optimism. It has enabled me to be fully myself – someone who wants to spread love everywhere, someone who believes that there is good in all people and that our prayers can be answered if we let go of defining how and when they will happen. Expressing Gratitude to this higher energy connects me with it, and brings me closer to *being* it - it activates divine energy within me. It also helps me become more aware of the layers upon layers of blessings within me, surrounding me and permeating my life both with and without my conscious contribution.

In Chapter 3, I will dive into the specific ways that Gratitude practice helps me on my spiritual journey, and how it has supported my healing journey and led me to be more open, grounded, balanced and connected to Source.

Cultivating Positive Experiences

As I mentioned earlier, I am on a mission to create a Positivity Bias. This means that as much as I possibly can, I consciously choose language in my thoughts and speech that aligns with the life I want - a positive, peaceful, joyful and loving one. On both my self-development and spiritual development journeys, I came upon the Law of Attraction, which has often felt like a useful tool to cultivate the positive life I intend for myself.

Many people I have met on my journey have appreciated the notion that "You get out what you put in", so the Law of Attraction is a concept I feel will be somewhat relatable to most. However, without the proper explanation, it can seem frustratingly oversimplified. I hope that by sharing my learnings around Gratitude practice for cultivating positive experiences, more people will be able to harness the Law of Attraction to bring more positive energy into their lives and into the world.

My interpretation of the Law of Attraction is the notion that you are creating your own reality by what you think about most and how you feel about it. According to the teachings I have seen around this, if you are only able to mostly think about how difficult life is and experience negative feelings, for example, you will experience life as mostly difficult.

I have been working with the Law of Attraction on and off for a few years now, and understand how it's been working for me, and not! I'm clearer about some of its principles, and have 'manifested', or magnetised as I prefer to call it, some amazing experiences, dream jobs and 'things'. However, my intention is to continue to cultivate this tool with compassion, as I have experienced some huge challenges and transformations in the last few years and appreciate that unless you are a true master of this modality, there are times in life when it can be very difficult to stick with it.

What I find very clear is that Law of Attraction teachers such as Abraham-Hicks, expertly channelled by Esther Hicks, highlight Gratitude as a key element to getting more of what you want in your life. Appreciating what is already yours and visualising being grateful for already having what you want - now **that** I can work with!

In Chapter 4, I address the benefits I've found in practising Gratitude to cultivate positive energy in my life experiences, including feeling part of an infinite Universe, uplifting my mood in order to attract a more positive life and providing a positive focus to soothe challenges.

Chapter 5 tells the story behind my desire to promote conscious volunteering through charity projects and the ensuing song "Make It Right - The Gratitude Song".

In Chapter 6, I offer some kindful suggestions for your own journey with Gratitude, including some ideas for how to stay kind to yourself and some games to bring more fun and play to your practice.

Chapter 7 is a 14 Day Challenge, running alongside a series of 14 vignettes, with invited reflections and practices to enrich your learning. The intention is to help you develop a habit of Gratitude over 14 days by reading a vignette, reflecting and engaging with the practices. The vignettes describe my personal journey and experiences of Gratitude, from my first mental health breakthrough, highlighting other notable wellbeing epiphanies, up until some of my most recent learning.

In Chapter 8, I share the conclusions of my one-woman experiment, where I am now with my practice, how it fits into my wellbeing strategy and some final thoughts for you to reflect on.

Now that you're starting to get a good idea of how Gratitude has helped me, I want to get something straight: what Gratitude practice is not!

When practising Gratitude, it's not about:

- Glossing over problems that require action, especially immediate action
- Forcing yourself to try to feel good when you're feeling really low
- Settling for less than you truly need
- Accepting poor service that leaves you inconvenienced, dissatisfied or your needs unmet (this is relative to each individual of course).

Let me offer you a recent example. A while back, I had a low-cost gym membership. At the beginning, my judgemental mind would pick holes in all the ways this gym was lacking, but eventually I changed my mindset to one of

Gratitude, remembering in particular that a friend of mine with severe mental and physical health challenges can only dream of this experience - my floor is his ceiling. What felt like a low experience for me was something he was reaching up for. Thanks to my mindset shifting to one of Gratitude, I had several months of really enjoying the classes. Even though my critical mind would occasionally still eagerly point out misgivings about the service, I was able to develop an attitude of Gratitude for the needs it was meeting and the benefits I was receiving.

Then an incident happened which resulted in me feeling unvalued, unwelcome and excluded as a customer. At first, I thought, I don't want to leave because I've done a great job of learning to appreciate it under some challenging circumstances. My Gratitude perspective had enabled me to make the best of a situation that was not ideal, and as a result I had been getting stronger and fitter. But the thought of going back there made my heart sink. Out of compassion to myself, I decided that I don't need to pay for a service where I feel like a second-class citizen, so I left.

In a nutshell, I offer the following as what practising Gratitude is:

- Maintaining a positive outlook on the world for yourself and for those around you, through gentle, welcoming invitations to new perspectives or practices

- Generating positive, tonic energy for yourself and those around you through genuine appreciation that arises naturally

- Soothing and guiding your mind to proactively seek out what's going right, especially when the going gets tough, but not so tough that you feel guilty for not being grateful

- Helping you stay calm, balanced and positive as much as possible, for better outcomes

- Expressing love and appreciation for the blessings and gifts in your life in personalised, sincere and meaningful ways, to whomever or whatever you believe is responsible for them, and that includes YOU!

- Feeling part of this awesome, infinite universe of possibilities and contributing to the mass of positive energy within it.

Kindful Reader Reflections

What would you like to get out of this book?

Write your intention on your bookmark or a post-it note to prompt a kind reminder while you're reading, and aid the specific learning or outcomes you're aiming for.

Chapter 2

Gratitude for Wellbeing

While there have been many quantitative studies showing how Gratitude practice has improved the wellbeing of those who dabble in it, I offer you this publication to share in detail the qualitative results of my one-woman study! As such, this chapter covers my personal learning from years of dabbling to eventual embedding and includes what I believe to be some new theories about it. These theories have been inspired from time in nature and meditation and I attribute them to the Divine Source speaking through me to uplift humanity and facilitate a much needed awakening. I am infinitely grateful for this, as I have watched humankind and the people around me suffer for many years, and I truly believe that what I have learnt can help.

Mental wellbeing, just like mental health, can be difficult to define, but I like mental health charity Mind's offering:

"Mental wellbeing doesn't have one set meaning. We might use it to talk about how we feel, how well we're coping with daily life or what feels possible at the moment.

Good mental wellbeing doesn't mean you're always happy. Or that you're unaffected by your experiences…. Poor mental wellbeing can make it more difficult to cope with daily life." (Mind, 2023)

I like to think of mental wellbeing as snapshots of my mental health's bigger picture, showing me how I'm feeling and how I'm experiencing life, segment by segment. When I take notice of these snapshots, it gives me a flavour of my whole life and I can make any adjustments needed in order to improve my experience of it and realign myself with the life I want to live. This requires regular tuning in, and Gratitude practice is a great companion here.

I worked with a client with complex mental health difficulties, including Post Traumatic Stress Disorder and Obsessive Compulsive Disorder and a history of trauma that had created a state of severe mental ill health for him. It crushed his independence and meant that he experienced a very limited life of being unable to do some of the most basic things that mentally well people do every day, like going to the shops or seeing friends. In general, his mental health was extremely poor as he suffered from illnesses and conditions that had created unhealthy and destructive beliefs and ensuing behaviours. But having had the privilege of working with him, I was able to witness his ability to experience moments of wellbeing. When he interacted with his cats, or when we did some very simple practices together, his motivation to work towards his recovery and a better life enabled him to be present with his pets and enjoy nourishing feelings. When the positive input stopped, however, he unconsciously returned to his default state of mental ill health. So while the wellbeing practice and pet interactions soothed his wellbeing, he still needed the proper treatment to deal with the root causes of the illness to ensure his long term mental health.

Life is a constant flow of energies and experiences, so our wellbeing changes from moment to moment. This is why I feel we need to make a conscious effort to be more aware of it than life naturally allows. It is because of the way this world works and my years of struggling with poor mental health that I now make my daily wellbeing a focus – this is a key strategy that I have put in place to ensure my own mental health, and Gratitude practice is a tool I find effective, uplifting and enjoyable. I must stress however, that Gratitude is only part of my wellbeing toolkit, and something that I practise kindfully – with mindfulness and kindness. I maintain awareness of how I am practising and if it is not coming from the heart, if it feels forced or difficult, I don't judge myself. Instead, I tune in to how I'm feeling, for example, through a Self-Care Check In (see the Pool of Practices chapter for the description).

Gratitude is a win-win double sided coin. It is both an uplifting and soothing strategy and I have found that it can also help naturally reprogramme some negative beliefs (it's great for mindsets around scarcity and lack, for example), but mental ill health often needs inner work or interventions from health professionals, just as my depression did. When you find the right ones for you, they can help you clear a path for more nourishing beliefs, thought patterns and behaviours, and improve your quality of life in the long term so that your daily wellbeing looks brighter and feels more robust.

That was the journey I took. I was unable to 'unstick myself' and lift the veil of depression myself, so I went through several stages of 'unsticking' with various professionals and programmes. These are covered in the daily readings of the 14 Day Challenge. After several breakthroughs, I had learnt my way out of the depression – but at the time, I could not have done it without outside help. That's not to say that no-one can – we are all unique and react and respond differently to life.

In the few years that I have been writing this book, I have still on occasion become aware of the onset of potentially depressive states. The differences now are:

1) I have noticed them early on and been able to navigate them with mental wellbeing practices, including Gratitude

2) I accept and love myself for being different

3) I am learning to let go of trying to 'fit in'.

My positive Gratitude wiring has truly helped me find a happy place in this world.

The more recent brushes with depression were very different to my initial one. To paint a picture, the first time I became depressed in 1993, it felt like I was on a very turbulent flight in the cargo hold of a rickety old aeroplane with no seat, let alone a seatbelt and some very rude, aggressive and unhelpful attendants. This time round, I was still on a difficult journey, but the plane had been completely upgraded, there were kind and helpful announcements about turbulence, the flight attendants were amazing and I was flying Business Class! Much better! I attribute this success partly to my embedded Gratitude habits.

There are many barriers to mental wellbeing, some are within our control, and some are not. Stress can have a paralysing impact on our daily wellbeing if we don't understand it or learn to manage it in the best ways for us.

One of the learnings that has amazed and helped me the most on my journey into mental wellbeing is some of the science behind stress - the Negativity Bias. Since the earliest ages of human life, our brains have been wired to seek out danger. In modern life, this is reflected in our tendency to seek out, focus on and remember the negative more than the positive. Sometimes the brain registers these as danger and responds to them as life or death situations – this is our 'Fight, Flight or Freeze' stress response. Stress manifests in people differently, but I fathom that most of you recognise some of the key physiological and mental symptoms in yourself such as tense muscles, shallow fast breathing and impaired memory and concentration. This response makes sense in the case of our primaeval ancestors, where ferocious wild animals roamed freely; if your stress response didn't kick in and activate your relevant physiological defence systems, in other words, your ability to run fast or fight effectively, you would most likely have been…consumed.

But in today's age, the Negativity Bias is reflected in our tendency to dwell on or be more deeply impacted by negative experiences than positive ones, even if in reality they are not threats at all. Let's say you're at work and you've just submitted an important presentation to your manager but you've not heard anything back. Your mind may start to jump to negative conclusions that it went down like a lead balloon, when the likelihood is that your manager has simply had to prioritise other things and delay feeding back to you about it.

Our wiring often assumes the worst and creates unnecessary stress within our whole being. For this reason, I believe it is also responsible for a lot of unnecessary stress, which is why I would like to offer my learnings around how Gratitude practice has helped me better maintain my wellbeing.

❖ **It can activate the Parasympathetic Nervous System, helping us to de-stress**

Life for our earliest ancestors may have revolved around more immediate threats than ours, but their lives were certainly simpler. The daily focus was along the lines of eat, avoid being eaten, hunt, sleep, repeat. It wasn't Instagram followers, mortgages, and certainly not their life purpose, it was survival.

While our inherent psychological wiring has remained the same, we no longer face daily threats of being gobbled up by sabre-toothed tigers et al. What our brains perceive as a threat may be different for everyone, for example, an argument with a partner or colleague or financial problems, but the common factor is that the brain sees it as a threat to life, and activates our stress response via the Sympathetic Nervous System (also known as the Threat System), to ensure our survival. This is essential for emergencies and actual threats to life (jumping back to avoid a swerving car etc.), and you probably notice some of the most obvious physical signs of it activating in stressful situations; faster, shallow breathing, rapid pulse, tension in your muscles.

Our stress response also evokes psychological effects. Our cognitive function is impaired, which can cause such symptoms as rigid thinking and poor judgement or decision making among others (Des Marais, 2022). This may be because "the primary function of our sympathetic nervous system is to keep your body safe from danger" (Olivine, 2023), so when it is activated, cognitive processes responsible for more complex tasks such as making decisions or judgements are relegated in favour of the simpler ones needed to move the body away from the threat or protect itself (the fight, flight or freeze response).

Here's a real life example: A while ago I was out of work and therefore living on the lower levels of the Maslow model. I was leaving my flat to get to an important appointment at the Job Centre, only to discover that builders had completely blocked our driveway, preventing me from accessing my car. My brain identified this as a threat because if I didn't get to the appointment, it could cause financial problems for my partner and I. This was a definite possibility but certainly not life threatening, yet my brain had jumped to the worst conclusions. Fight or flight kicked in and I went from 0 to fuming in seconds, focusing on fighting for my need to be able to get out and on the road immediately. What I realised only after I was calm again and on my way to the appointment, was that I had known there was another way through! I could have walked round the back of the communal gardens quite easily, accessed my car from there, and been home free with no dramas whatsoever (except for maybe some brambly hair styling). But my brain 'forgot' that – I was in survival mode instead of solution mode.

And that's the point – this wiring is for survival.

Our stress response was only meant to protect us for short periods of time, to get out of life-threatening situations. Once the threat is deemed to be gone, normal service is resumed. This relies upon the brain being satisfied that the danger is over – and in modern day situations, this may not happen while you are, for example, in an environment, situation or relationship where the stressors continue to affect you.

So, while our higher cognitive functioning is benched in order to 'preserve life', we are left in stressful situations with diminished mental capabilities such as problem-solving – the kind that would really come in handy, say, if we were in a stressful situation and needed some creative solutions! While we may have evolved enough to come up with some very creative solutions to world problems, our wiring has yet to adapt to this modern life of stressful yet non-life threatening situations.

With this awareness lighting the way, we can find ways to develop a grounded and grateful mindset along with some key practices as a powerful pacifier of our overactive Threat System. Of course, this comes with the caveat that if there is an actual threat or danger, our Threat System is there to guide us to survival.

The challenge is, however, that it will stay active until the brain is happy that the threat has passed. With ongoing stressful situations, this can leave us feeling stressed and exhausted for extended periods, unless we proactively override our Threat System by activating our Parasympathetic Nervous System (our Soothe System). Gratitude practice can be an excellent tool if you notice that you've been feeling stressed and want to rebalance for a more peaceful experience and clearer mind.

❖ **It can generate tonic emotions such as peacefulness, calmness, happiness and contentment, which block unpleasant emotions like frustration and anger, that can become toxic if suppressed**

When I was first diagnosed with depression at university, I was prescribed a series of Cognitive Behavioural Therapy sessions. In retrospect, I can see that I was too young and too entrenched in the condition to be able to gain any real benefit from it, except for understanding this:

Thoughts create feelings.

I have developed a level of self-awareness that helps me leverage this to great effect. I've learnt to notice the early signs of stress, emotional wobbling and the potential for being knocked off balance. I tune in to the thoughts that are at play underneath the surface - ooh boy can they be sneaky! I'll often find that there are judgments that I was unaware of, and as soon as I tune in and kindly deal with them, the thoughts improve and my mood lifts.

That's not to say that it's wholly our fault if we are constantly thinking thoughts that bring us down – they can come from so many different sources. We can only take responsibility and helpful action if we are **aware** that we are thinking them, and self-awareness is a skill you develop over time.

Experiencing the full range of emotions is part of human life, even the unpleasant, uncomfortable or 'negative' ones. By the time my depression hit, I had developed a habit of judging emotions such as sadness and anger as 'bad', and worse still, that I was a bad person for feeling them. Any time they arose, I would spiral into very low moods as I had no healthy strategies to deal with them.

Nowadays I strive to welcome all emotions as I have found that they always bring a message that helps me. For years, however, I looked for just one key thing that would help me get back to feeling happy or 'OK' in any given situation, no matter how bad it was. Gratitude is definitely a key player, but on my own journey into maintaining my wellbeing I discovered that it's about having a **set** of keys and learning which ones are effective in which emotional states or situations. Most importantly for my work with Gratitude, if I'm feeling too low, I just can't appreciate the 'food on the table' because I don't feel emotionally safe. Gratitude can be the furthest thing from my mind – but you know what?

That's OK! I'm human.

What is evident to me, is that once I developed Gratitude habits and regular practices that I enjoy, they've become like muscles fuelling my resilience. When mild to moderate challenges pop up, in general, my Gratitude mindset deflects them quite quickly and easily. When more intense or higher impact challenges arise, I know that I have a Gratitude toolkit to use, but my self-awareness will make an assessment of what perspective is best for me: Am I able to see the silver lining yet and get on with the solution or do I need some kindness first?

In these circumstances, there can be a dance of thoughts and emotions. A part of me will want to 'get to the good stuff', i.e the happier feelings, but my intuition will prompt me to deal with the uncomfortable ones because it knows they can only be released if I deal with them. Either way, once I am able to turn to Gratitude, I find myself feeling calmer, more peaceful and even happy.

❖ It can offer a new perspective during times where we feel stuck

There have been times when I could not get past a negative mindset in a situation, as I was constantly ruminating. I asked myself, what new thoughts can I find around this situation? I need a different perspective. And Gratitude just slid in, as if it had been waiting in the wings! It worked beautifully as I only asked what I felt *able* to feel grateful for, there was no demanding or judgement, and no expectation that this would solve the problem itself, just my thinking around it, and as a result, it soothed my thoughts and uplifted my feelings.

- ❖ **When every day things break down or 'go wrong', it can help counteract and de-escalate 'awfulising' disaster thoughts and clear a path for more level-headed, solution focused thinking**

I can speak from personal experience that rewiring my brain to look for things I can appreciate has significantly helped me to stay balanced during potentially stressful situations, built my resilience and helped me maintain a positive outlook. I'm still human, of course, and still learning to balance positive focus with realistic action! But to take a few practical examples, when there's a petrol crisis, a power cut, the water supply stops, or even when my laptop has gone wobbly, I am not one of those people panic buying or getting stressed. I'm able to smile to myself and feel grateful that **this is not my normal**, and then make mindful plans to resolve the situation. It's important to note here that the above is my response during 'business as usual' times, when I am balanced and resilient. The example I gave earlier, where I got stressed thinking I might miss my appointment at the Job Centre took place during a time of extended unemployment, among other intense life challenges. It was taking a lot of my resources to get up in the morning and keep going while money was depleted, so understandably this situation caused my stress bucket to overflow a little. At times like these, I call upon Gratitude's sibling, Kindness, and apply it generously in recognition of my being human! If you're interested in self-kindness practice, my Self-Care Check In technique is a good place to start.

❖ **When practised regularly, it can help counteract the Negativity Bias, our survival-focused, threat-seeking wiring, and retrain our brains to actively seek out and focus on the positive**

One of the things I remember most about being depressed was how it stole my ability to bounce back – my resilience. My mind would respond to even small things as disasters – I've found that this can also be common for some mentally well people who have a lot on their plates and have not yet learnt to manage stress. When I was depressed though, it was my default state. I was unable to cope with disappointments as I had no control over the constant judgement of myself, which just drove me deeper and deeper into a pit of despair, with no glimmer of hope or light.

What I didn't know at the time, but would learn through a course called The Phil Parker Lightning Process® (LP) created by Dr. Phil Parker, is that aside from the daily challenges of being human, we have this sneaky subconscious wiring at work - the Negativity Bias (Rozin and Royzman, 2001). Not only is our brain looking out for 'threats' to our survival, but it is also seeking out all the negative experiences! This is intensified by much of what is shared in the news and on social media day in and day out. In fact, the constant negative focus in the media may even be a systemic example of how the Negativity Bias is showing up in our human world!

Think about it, in all the conversations you have with friends, family, colleagues, even strangers you encounter in your daily life, how often do you hear people talking about the things that have gone right or well, and how often do you hear them sharing about the difficulties, the things that went wrong, the judgements of themselves or of others? Perhaps you've been for an interview or delivered a presentation - do you find that you remember the things you weren't happy with or that you felt could have gone better? These are examples of how the Negativity Bias is active in our thinking. But talking about this stuff is only one way of dealing with it! Of course it's good to talk, but we need to be aware of the things that influence our thinking - this has been one of the most powerful learnings of my life.

We can choose what to think!

As I started to choose to think more positively, more thankfully, more in the present, my mindset changed. As my mindset changed, I found that my words changed. As my words changed, my conversations changed (inside and out!). As my conversations changed, my **experiences** changed!

But what I'm talking about is not Toxic Positivity, where you suppress, reject or avoid negative emotions or experiences. It's not glossing over things that need attention with a big daub of "everything's fine".

It's finding a better way to use our brains for a better life.

It took me several years to train my brain to jump to more positive conclusions. Firstly through the Phil Parker

Lightning Process® course, at which point I started to magnetise a whole host of positive people from the personal development world. This was an affirmation that I was on the right track, as my inner positivity was being reflected back to me through these new experiences.

As I became more positive though, I began to notice the contrast of people around me suffering and struggling with life's ups and downs. It was only then that I realised that I was no longer one of them. I felt a little like the subject of Rudyard Kipling's iconic poem, "If" – I was able to keep my head while those around me were struggling to. But this was not just about keeping my head, it was about keeping my heart….open! My empathy for these people was the fuel behind setting up Highest Good Wellbeing, and the reason I ran free workshops and projects throughout lockdown - my new way of actively paying my Gratitude forward.

I have found that practising Gratitude for Wellbeing is most effective as part of my 3 Keys to Wellbeing approach:

- Self-Awareness
- Self-Kindness
- Self-Nourishment.

If you're not aware that your wellbeing is wobbling, how can you possibly help stabilise it?

And if you're not kind enough to yourself to take time out, however little, to nourish yourself, how can you enjoy wellbeing, and life in general?

The physical benefits of practising Gratitude are harder for me to quantify and prove, but I can say with certainty that I've never felt calmer and more peaceful in my life than in the last few years. What I'm feeling physically, according to the rare studies on this, is lower blood pressure and the deactivation of my stress response. I believe this has also contributed to my robust health, even after my encounter with a now not very mysterious virus in early 2020… In essence, my practices, including Gratitude, help me manage stress so I enjoy a feeling of physical and mental wellbeing more of the time.

If you suffer with daily health challenges, my heart goes out to you. In such cases it can be difficult to access Gratitude as a wellbeing technique. Everyone is different, and sadly many people suffer from chronic and serious illnesses, while others have permanent disabilities or impairments as part of their daily life. I would never expect anyone to practise Gratitude in the same way as I do, in fact, my hope for this book is that it will inspire you to take or continue your own journey, in your own way. I was unaware of how much I used to take my health for granted, until 'that virus' came knocking on my door. The way it affected my chest and lungs meant that I could not turn to my Stress Management go-to – breathing practice. Since that experience, I find myself sometimes pausing just to enjoy taking a few breaths and the ease with which they flow. Appreciating this freedom nourishes me emotionally, in addition to the physical nourishment I receive from the purposeful breaths.

Bearing in mind the benefits I have discussed above, I invite you to try one of the exercises from the Pool of Practices chapter. I recommend the Gratitude Hierarchy or Gratitude Inventory for this particular section to see if you feel any of the benefits I have mentioned, or perhaps some others. To help measure the effect of the practice on your wellbeing, you could do a Self-Care Check In before you start, and record how you're feeling. You could then repeat it after the practice to see how the practice has affected you, if at all.

Kindful Reader Reflections

How do you feel about your wellbeing?

At this stage of the book, do you get a sense of how Gratitude could nourish your wellbeing?

If so, how? If not, take some time to kindfully reflect on the resistance you may have around improving your wellbeing through learning about and practising Gratitude.

Chapter 3

Gratitude for Spiritual Journey

Spirituality is unique to everyone and can often be dismissed as too weird, "woo woo" or 'out there' to add any real value for the realities of human life. Here's why I beg to differ.

To me, spirituality is about:

- Aligning with Source energy as much as possible - essentially **being love** and doing my best to bring love to all situations. This involves practising to consciously generate, cultivate, engage with and radiate the best possible energy in everything I do, using the highest, most loving and nourishing thoughts, words and actions I can. This requires an acceptance and recognition that humans are by nature susceptible to negative energy, whereas the Divine Source transcends it, as it is pure love.

- Letting go of resistance (for example, thoughts and feelings about needing myself and things to be a certain way), to 'just be' and experience higher thoughts that come from a pure source of positive energy, of love.

- Tuning in to the unique essence of my soul, my gifts and my purpose in order to fulfil my highest service to the planet and fulfil my potential, my Self-Actualisation.

- Leaning in to and allowing myself to experience my blockages, life lessons and challenges in order to face them and heal them, which clears away barriers to my Self-Actualisation.

- Connecting with my Higher Self (my best self, almost like a future me) or my Highest Intelligence (what I believe is a part of my mind that is not limited by human thought and is directly connected to Source), higher energies and guides to receive their guidance and support in fulfilling my purpose and Self-Actualisation.

- Being part of the collective effort of healers and lightworkers focusing their energies on healing the world by raising the vibration of this planet to one of love, peace and unity for Mother Earth herself, for those who are struggling and for the longer term goal of peace.

There is a lot more underneath all this, but in essence, I believe that the spiritual path is about being the best I can be, and doing everything in alignment with this loving, higher energy I call Source. It is also a uniquely personal journey and it's therefore vital to learn to be resilient and unshakeable in knowing and feeling what is right for you - to follow your own divine inner teacher and no-one else. Furthermore, I believe that it is a path for alleviating suffering, but not through further suffering or struggle - through aligned service and from a full cup filled with good energy.

I have learnt that if I want a higher life, a life where I am on the path to Self-Actualisation, my highest service to the planet, and flourishing through that, I need to actually be **in** that higher energy as much as possible. I need to create time and space to connect with it and to receive guidance that helps me find a bridge to solutions to my challenges and to things that may feel impossible.

To take one example of things that have felt impossible in my life, I had a dream to complete my degree after dropping out of university with depression. Through meditation, Gratitude, connection to Source and support and encouragement from loved ones, I was able to befriend my academic demons of 'not good enough' and perfectionism. Through both my spiritual (and wellbeing) practices, I was able to identify and transform the limiting beliefs that had, until then, prevented me from completing my degree. It was Gratitude, in fact, that helped me with my perfectionism in the end, as it helped me focus on how far I'd come, and how amazing it was that I was actually an undergraduate student on her way to becoming a graduate. Focusing on the level I was studying at, the fact that I got to choose what to study, learn about things that made me come alive (like language and writing) and develop skills that I'd been longing to for years, helped me let go of trying to get full marks all the time, and I completed it with a 2:1 with Honours.

To me, Gratitude is the vibration of "All is well. I have everything I need" which I believe echoes the vibration of Source, so when I align myself with that vibration, I feel peaceful, loving and abundant - I feel Divine!

Practising Gratitude as part of my spiritual routine has led me to seek growth beyond the material gain of being successful in order to acquire more 'things' and 'stuff'. It has seeded in me the desire to pay forward my Gratitude to humanity in fulfilling my potential and helping uplift others - you can read about the first time I heard the inner calling to my purpose during my earliest stages of depression in Day 5 of the 14 Day Challenge.

Gratitude as part of my spiritual practice helps me in the following ways:

❖ It helps me open my heart more

When I began my spiritual journey, the teachers I encountered were always saying, "Open your heart," when challenges or 'blockages' came up for me or their other students. At first, I found this frustrating as I did not know what it meant in practice. My human mind would be searching for something to *do* to solve and fix it. Over the years, I have come to understand that for me, it's an invitation to let go of any or all of the following and more:

- Needing to solve everything now

- Needing to have all the answers now or ever
- Needing to know how I will receive what I need or want
- Needing to be right
- Perfection

It is also about:

- Being open to receiving in ways I can and cannot imagine
- Trusting that I am always taken care of by a higher energy
- Having an open mind about the reasons things happen

Letting go of the above limitations has brought me the freedom of new thoughts, experiences and solutions, and Gratitude practice is key to creating such an environment in your mind. It brings me into the present moment and delving into the countless miracles of all that is right with my world connects me with the limitless nature of the Divine Source and the Universe in which I reside. This acts as a bridge to letting go of limitations and mindsets that might block good things from coming to me. By letting go of limitations, I have found that I am creating a great big space in which to embrace new and nourishing solutions, beliefs and ideas.

Take this example: I was looking for a job but hated the thought of doing more sedentary or office based work.

Instead of focusing my practice and prayers on not working in an office, I asked to find work that made me happy, and tried to let go of the what, how and when. A few weeks later, I got a job as a Kids' Exercise Coach! What is more amazing about this, is that, since the age of 15, when the depression was setting in, I had started dreaming of becoming a P.E Teacher or Fitness Instructor. At the time, I was diagnosed with a knee condition that I was told would prevent this from happening. Long story short, despite doing my best to overcome the apparent obstacle to my dream career through Physiotherapy and whatever mental strength I could muster during the deepest phases of the depression, I never made it over the line. So when I got the job as a Kids' Exercise Coach, I was absolutely elated! Source had finally found a way for my dream to come true, just not in a way or timescale that I had expected - 30 or so years later and working with kids in nurseries! I could not have imagined that even though my dream had felt completely out of reach back then, that I would find a way of being a Fitness Instructor without the intensity of being a full time instructor and at the higher levels of knee pressure required to work with adults.

By opening my heart more through Gratitude practice, creative solutions to what I want have flowed into my life in surprising and inspiring ways. With this, I have found myself so grateful for the 'coincidences' and things that were clearly meant to be. This has led to me pouring love out into the world through my thoughts, words, actions and projects – fulfilling my purpose! Gratitude has helped me move myself up the hierarchy of needs, into self-actualisation!

❖ It helps me stay grounded when things come up to be healed

The spiritual path, contrary to the belief of those who are unfamiliar with it or do not follow one, is not all sunshine and rainbows. It takes courage, patience and building up robust resilience through personalised practices in order to withstand the continuous 'shakes of the snowglobe' as I like to call it. What I'm referring to is the steps on the path that require you to make pattern-breaking choices, to truly look your fears and blockages in the eye. Some people call it testing, others 'purification'. For me, these are the greatest growth opportunities, but they are often emotionally difficult experiences as we are being asked to challenge old beliefs and conditioning that may have kept us feeling safe for years, and that can feel like someone is 'shaking your snowglobe'!

Here, Gratitude is a great place to call home.

It serves as a 'go to' practice for when things come up to be healed and feel painful or distressing. It may not always be the first thing I am able to reach for, as with my wellbeing experiences, but certainly once the ground shaking has begun to settle, it is a nourishing way to re-centre and rebalance myself and see the good that is coming from guiding myself through these difficult and uncomfortable experiences. Once again, I see Gratitude and its sibling Kindness skipping happily together in this context, as well as the wellbeing context; Gratitude is not something to be forced - on oneself or anyone else.

I find that the more I have practised it, the more 'breadcrumbs' I have left myself that lead me back to why I am on this path and why I am choosing to do this inner work. These 'breadcrumbs' return me to a state of trust and faith that everything will work out for the best.

❖ It cultivates humility by helping me understand that I am one part of something much bigger

As Gratitude became part of my spiritual furniture, it opened me up to the limitless possibilities of a higher energy supporting me and guiding me. When I first started out on my journey with Gratitude, I did a bit of a dance with the 'Thank who?' side of things, but opening my heart and letting go of trying to figure everything out has felt more nourishing than trying to pin down a definitive answer. Moreover, spiritual Gratitude practice can evoke a sense of curiosity and wonder.

Let's take the example of being grateful for being able to eat fresh fruit and vegetables. On the one hand, my partner and I are the ones who work to earn the money to buy them. However, I see that there is much more to it than just money in the bank. It feels to me like a beautiful team effort of good energy from many directions, some of which I can pinpoint, and some less so or not at all.

- The Earth works in harmony with nature to provide the energy, nurturing environment and nutrients for these living things to grow and flourish into something we can fuel ourselves with

- Farmers and other workers grow the produce and bring it to market
- A whole host of organisations, people, equipment, systems and processes energy and power is needed to deliver the food to the shop shelves
- Another whole host of organisations, people, equipment, systems, processes, energy and power enables the shop to sell the produce.

It is clear who and what are responsible for these things.

But what about the freedom and independence we have to go to the shop, to choose what to eat, the health and physical and mental capacity we have to cook them as part of a meal?

What about the fact that I had the good fortune of being born in a developed country where these nutritious foods are so readily available? Where having a fridge is the norm?

What about the good fortune I had to have been brought up in a wonderful family, with incredible opportunities to educate and develop myself to the point where I am independent?

What about my health? Who and what are truly responsible for all of that?

These are huge questions! For the purposes of this book, I shall just say this:

Developing an awareness of the absolute goldmine of gifts and blessings happening in my life every day has led me to believe that I am in fact working as a team with this higher energy some people call God, and that is an amazingly comforting and uplifting notion for me. If you asked me to prove it, I wouldn't be able to (although in future books I may talk about some of the amazing experiences I have had), but I feel it in my energy and the more I feel it, the more my feeling becomes knowing. The more this knowing becomes faith, the more I see my inner world transform, my physical world start to improve and my experiences become more beautiful and enjoyable.

A real life example I can offer is that when I last took my car for a service, I was told that his rear brake pads and discs needed replacing, but not immediately. This was going to cost a few hundred pounds, which I would struggle to cover. I was also told that, having examined the electric window mechanism that was not working, the whole thing would need to be replaced, costing another couple of hundred pounds. I decided to have faith and invest the money I had available into the former job, but my spiritual self also felt that it would be a way of showing my Gratitude to my car, which has served me so well. As it turned out, when I tried the window a few days later, it was working! To me, it felt like my car had felt the Gratitude and investment of my financial energy, and healed itself! There is no way to prove what was truly responsible for this miracle, but I am certainly grateful that it happened and it gives me hope that the good energy and heartfelt nature in which I live my life is reverberating into my physical experience!

All of the above have led me to a greater relationship with Source. I feel more connected and able to trust that there will always be good energy for me whenever I call upon it through connection, thoughts, intentions, prayer or practice.

Kindful Reader Reflections:

Look at one thing you need to do every day in your life – can you identify all the people, things, equipment, energies and sub-processes involved in creating just one of these processes in your life? Feel free to do this on a separate piece of paper if you wish!

If you can't home in one, try choosing something simple, like making a hot drink. Try creating a visual representation of this one process in a way that feels enjoyable to you. Perhaps a colourful mind map, a picture, a list, a poem or even a dance!

If you feel called to take this a step further, you could explore your connection with the elements of this process. What is your relationship with each one like? How does it feel?

Chapter
4

Gratitude for Cultivating Positive Experiences

I have found that practising Gratitude for wellbeing and my spiritual journey has indeed contributed to the Positivity Bias I decided to create for myself, and that I hope ripples out into the world. Everything I have shared in the previous two chapters has cultivated more positive experiences in my life, but not just in those two areas.

Positive experiences can feel out of reach for some, especially those who have been stuck in very difficult situations for so long that it may feel impossible for them to entertain thoughts of life being any other way. I believe that mastering the Law of Attraction only works if you are able to feel the experience of **what you want and where you want to be**, regardless of **what you currently have and where you currently are**. So if you are struggling to have your basic needs met and are somewhere on the lowest levels of the Hierarchy of Needs, it can be incredibly difficult to imagine yourself higher up.

Here are some of my learnings around practising Gratitude to magnetise positive experiences:

❖ It plugs me in to the Universal energy

Through practising Gratitude, I feel connected to everyone and everything. I feel I can instantly connect to all that is good in my life and all that is provided in it. I feel taken care of by this good, kind, higher energy that I feel is Divine. This has opened me up to the limitless possibilities of a Divine Source, since my life is no longer limited to what my human, protective mind can fathom.

At the beginning of my journey with Gratitude, it inspired me to start a sandwich making club for the homeless which cultivated nearly 10 years of positive experiences. You can read about it in the 14 Day Challenge in Chapter 7. But I can offer a more recent example of writing a song about Gratitude (see Chapter 5 for the full story). I felt an overwhelming sense of Gratitude for my basic needs being met with barely any effort from me, and this inspired me to pour that into the practice of writing a song about it. I had no idea at the time that I would, through universal synchronicity, meet my amazing and musically talented friend Geri O'Regan, who would join hearts with me to bring it to life and that we would perform it all over the place - from Buddhist temples, homeless charities, schools and personal development groups to community cafés and picnics, pubs, radio shows, the Museum of Happiness and even Steinway Hall. We would always marvel gratefully at the big smiles and hearty applause we received. "Everything about the song has brought me joy," says Geri, "From the words that are written in it, the joy of singing it, people's reactions and the experience of where the song has taken us."

The practice of allowing the good energy of Gratitude to flow through me and develop into something that touched people's hearts and made them smile is a great example of how Gratitude has connected me with the Universal energy that wants to bring people together and love them. Feeling part of a kind, loving and limitless Universe makes me feel kind, loving and limitless. I feel truly blessed to see and feel people light up and respond to our song in such positive ways. Life has more meaning because it's no longer just about me, or about a struggle to survive. It's about being part of nature, part of an intricate and beautiful work of art, or a symphony, and being myself contributes to its shape and meaning.

These are just examples of where my heart has taken me. Your heart is unique, and so too will your journey be. I wonder what will flow through you, dear Reader, as you explore your journey with Gratitude.

❖ It elevates my vibration

You may have heard the term "good vibes" - emotions carry specific vibrations that resonate within us and affect our mood. 'Negative' or unpleasant ones, such as anger or sadness, have lower vibrations and 'positive' or more pleasant ones, such as happiness or Gratitude, have higher vibrations. Focusing on what's going right within me and all around me as much as I can uplifts my mood to a state where I am radiating a clear positive signal to the Universe (and to people around me), without resistance, that transmits messages such as "I know that all is well", "I feel lucky to be where I am" or "I feel happy with what I have". This is especially nourishing when things don't turn out as expected and those 'negative' emotions can arise. Many times where I have been out somewhere, feeling grateful for the privilege of just being out and among friends, and although something might have gone wrong with the experience, for example a meal, it has smoothed itself out through positive and grateful interactions with staff.

Since developing this mindset of Gratitude, I feel the benefit of it more now when I go out. This is partly because I have not been able to go out a lot recently, but it is also because I feel a warmth in my heart around service and I no longer see spending money on going out as just a form of transaction. I see it as an opportunity to experience more of what life has to offer, which includes the privilege of being served by others.

As you explore your own journey with Gratitude, I invite you to start noticing, with kindness, how practising it affects your vibration, how you feel, and any positive experiences that may arise.

❖ It can create a positive, upward spiral

The Negativity Bias, along with countless other attributes of human life, can make it easy for us to focus on what's missing from our lives and swing into low mood if we're not aware enough to catch it. I have found that making time to think about the parts of my life that satisfy my needs and allowing myself to linger and enjoy this can overturn low mood effectively and quickly. One day I noticed negative thinking creeping in and when I checked in with myself using my Needs Check-In Chart© (see the image in Chapter 5), I realised that I was actually feeling down about many areas of my life. This was during a period of unemployment and illness, so it was easy to slip into a focus on what was making me unhappy, because money and health come under the two most basic of our needs, Physiological and Safety needs respectively. When these needs feel jeopardised, it can affect our whole life perspective - it's almost as if the genre of our life movie changes from perhaps comfortably up and down comedy drama to scary, out of control thriller or even horror. Once I spotted this gloomy outlook and realised that it wasn't what I wanted for myself, I sat down and asked myself:

Which parts of my life AM I satisfied with? Where am I **starting** to make some progress? Are there **parts** of my life I can feel grateful for?

I found that by using the words **'starting'** and **'parts'**, I liberated myself from perfection and judgement! I was surprised and happy to find many areas I was making progress in and many parts I could be grateful for. Just like that, I turned a gloomy outlook into a brighter and kinder one. I felt relief and gratitude about my life in general. The negative thoughts were soothed and my vibration was smoothed out from inflamed anxiety and impatience to one of calmer contentment and even excitement about what else was to come.

❖ It can generate a feeling of abundance

Gratitude practice can simply mean paying attention to the abundance in my life. For example, doing my morning practice outside, I find myself giving thanks to Mother Earth for every blade of grass, every leaf on every tree and plant, every petal on every flower, every droplet of water in every ocean, every wisp of air that nourishes my body and mind and even all the ecosystems I know nothing about that are ensuring life on earth. Thinking about the infinite providence of these things expands my inner vision and I can see and feel beyond my current circumstances. That helps me feel more abundant and relaxed about life, knowing that there is plenty of what I need, even if some of it is not yet in my physical reality. This can also work with all the resources I have and what they allow me to do, for example, all the equipment in my office, all the clothes I have, all the dishes in our kitchen, all the books on my shelf and so on.

However, while this kind of practice is good for soothing the mind, which is focused on survival, exploring my intangible abundance can really nourish and open my heart. I may reflect and meditate to recall all the positive steps I have taken to get myself to where I am, appreciate all the freedoms and independence I have, all aspects of my health and the gifts they bring me, the love that comes to me from various sources and more.

❖ It supports my practice of pouring in positive 'information' to balance out and dissolve negative 'information'

Information is everywhere. It's all around us and within us and is being transmitted to us all the time from other people, organisations, videos, music, news, devices, even the food we eat, and if we believe and are attuned to it, higher energies like Source, Mother Earth and nature. On my wellbeing journey, I have learnt that actively seeking out the positive information all around me connects me and fills me with the good energy it brings. Everything is energy, so even our thoughts, words and actions carry energy which affects our own personal energy, the energy of others and ultimately the energy in the world. By consciously choosing positive information as much as possible, in what I think, say and do, I feel positive energy within me, my mood lifts and as such I have more positive experiences and interactions. This learning was reinforced and developed when I became a Tao Hands healing practitioner through the teachings of the modality's founder, Dr and Master Zhi Gang Sha. In his book, Tao Science, he talks about the Law of Information Energy Matter (the Law of Shen Qi Jing) stating that, "...everyone and everything is made of shen (information), energy and matter" and that "Information is the possibilities and possible states of an entity" (Sha & Xiu, 2017, p.46). What I have learnt from Master Sha has added an extra layer to my Positivity Bias and I am deeply grateful to him as it has nourished my practice and my life.

By operating on an attitude of Gratitude as much as possible, I am balancing out negative information, and therefore energy, within me and around me, which goes beyond just lifting my mood - it attracts positive energy and experiences. For example, I used to eat out at restaurants regularly before my journey into self-employment and part time work required more modest budgeting. I remember the times I experienced a lack of customer satisfaction, or being with others who experienced it, and how that dampened the pleasure of eating out. Since developing this mindset of Gratitude, I feel it more now when I go out. This is partly because I don't get to do it so often, but it is also because I now feel a warmth in my heart around service and I no longer see spending money on going out as just a transaction. I see it as an opportunity to experience more of what life has to offer, which includes the privilege of being served by others. As such, if the experience isn't flowing as hoped or expected these days, I find myself focusing on feeling grateful for the ability to be out. That radiates out to those around me and I enjoy more positive experiences and interactions.

❖ **It 'fills my cup' with good energy**

Since my spiritual awakening in 2015, I have been learning that in order to give my greatest service to the world, I need to keep my 'cup' of life topped up with good energy. To put it another way, I now accept that taking care of myself is an essential part of my serving the world, including my loved ones, from my heart and with my best energy. Burning myself out, however, is **not** part of it!

The positive outlook and nourishing thinking that arise in me naturally as a result of my embedded Gratitude mindset, contribute to my foundation of wellbeing. Now that it has become a habit for me, even a lifestyle, I know that it's there whenever I need some good energy. It naturally cultivates positive energy in me, and in situations, whenever I connect with it. Here's one example: If I've had a challenging or hectic day, when I sit down to eat and connect with all the energies that have enabled me to be experiencing my meal in freedom and health, I am able to slow down, be present with and truly enjoy my meal. A calmness comes over me and I relax back into my true loving self.

Gratitude literally fills my 'cup' as it brings my attention to what's actually 'in it', those blessings and gifts I may have forgotten about but don't need my attention to exist and bless me (any of my senses that are working well, the walls of my home or the air that I breathe for instance). From that place of feeling 'full', that many of my needs are taken care of, I feel more open and able to give of myself and be kind and positive experiences flow. You might notice this in your own life, perhaps when you are driving somewhere and not in a rush, it can feel much easier to be kind and giving and let other drivers go in front of you - you see their rush as stress and want to help them, and you are able to because you are not struggling, your cup at that moment feels full, life feels OK. It is wonderful to notice the part that Gratitude plays for me particularly in interactions with others - it can sometimes provide a bridge to kindness.

When the energy of Gratitude fills my life, it feels like I am choosing to write it in the feel-good genre.

Kindful Reader Reflections:

Are there any areas in your life that you would like to cultivate more positive energy and experiences?

Take a look at the Pool of Practices chapter to see if any of them call to you to help you practise Gratitude and change the energy around that area of your life. Remember to include kindness in your practice, so start with an area that's not too difficult and be kind to yourself if it gets uncomfortable.

Chapter

5

Your Floor Could Be Someone's Ceiling

"The thing you're looking down at and struggling to appreciate, could be the thing someone else aspires to have, a goal that is out of reach – they would love to have your Wifi issues or your shabby cupboards, or your mediocre meal, because for them, that would be better than having none at all."

Revisiting Maslow's Hierarchy of Needs, I feel extremely fortunate that all my basic needs are always met, and always have been. I've had some close calls and some experiences where the bottom rung of the hierarchy has felt unstable or unsafe, but that foundation always returned, and I count myself as privileged to be cruising between the top levels of the chart. I am blessed with the freedom to be able to focus mostly on my purpose and how to deliver it in the best possible way for humanity.

Maslow's hierarchy of needs

Source: www.simplypsychology.org With kind permission from Saul McLeod PhD

There are some days when I have struggled to feel emotionally safe and that drop can **feel** as if nothing else is going right, like I was right down at the bottom of the pyramid. When some of those basic needs have felt jeopardised, I've noticed that it would start to skew my whole outlook and impair my wellbeing.

It's those days that the embedded habits, my Gratitude muscles, show their strength. The habits of going to sleep and waking up with an outlook of Gratitude, of pausing before my meals to appreciate them, to seek out the learning or the blessing in a situation wherever possible (even after crying about it!) have trained my brain that this is now the norm, the norm which is creating a happier, more balanced life.

It's hard enough knowing that we have neighbours in developing countries who struggle with basic needs such as food and water, but I also recognise that even in developed countries like the UK, there are people having these kinds of experiences. The words I hear in my mind whenever I offer someone on the street a hot drink or some food is, "But I get to go home." If we're paying attention, we might experience fleeting fractions of what it's like to live on the bottom level of the Hierarchy of Needs. Waiting for public transport in winter, for example, is a situation where we have no control over when we will be in the warm again. Of course it does not remotely compare to a life on the street, being forced to live out in the cold with no shelter. In that moment, revisiting where you are on the Hierarchy of Needs can evoke a perspective of Gratitude and help you soothe stress by reminding you that this is only a temporary experience for you. My journey with Gratitude has helped me develop an awareness of these things and I am determined to continue paying my Gratitude forward in any way I can.

During my first attempt at university I was deep in depression, so it's no wonder that I didn't retain or use much of what I learnt. Maslow's Hierarchy of Needs was one concept that really stuck with me, though. After I broke out of the depression and began channelling my gratitude into Club Sandwich, my charity project making sandwiches for the homeless, it haunted me how lucky I was to be able to pursue my purpose so easily, when there were people who were stuck at the bottom of this hierarchy, struggling everyday to have their most basic needs met.

What about *their* Self-Actualisation?

It was this perspective that fuelled the development of Club Sandwich to Club Gratitude. I didn't want people to just come in and enjoy a social gathering while making sandwiches. I wanted them to appreciate the gift of giving – to be in a position to have free time and energy that they didn't need to spend on fighting for their basic needs, and consciously use that time and energy to support someone who was fighting for theirs. My dream is to take this further, and my hope is that by publishing this book, I will gather a community of like-hearted people and the resources to give consciously from an overflowing cup of great energy! It's unthinkable to me that there should be people with piles of spare money lying around, who don't have to give a second thought about their basic needs, while there are others whose only certainty is where their next breath is coming from.

Gandhi inspired me to "Be the change" I wish to see in the world, and this is one change I wish to see - no-one left behind. So that's my plan, to self-actualise by continuing the work I started and develop it into new higher impact, more sustainable projects with more conscious volunteering.

One way to keep myself grounded in Gratitude for the privilege of living on the higher levels of the Maslow's Hierarchy of Needs pyramid is through volunteering, which I did with various homeless charities at the beginning of my journey with Gratitude. However, I've recently found what feels like a more meaningful way to volunteer, by actually working with and trying to personally support people living on the bottom levels in developing countries, people who do not have government help or access to vital infrastructure. Through my work as a Tao Hands healing practitioner, I am grateful to be part of a community of heart-centred souls who truly wish to serve the world, not just through prayer and spiritual practice, but through providing physical and practical help wherever possible, and this includes communities in developing countries. Through these connections, I have become part of a working group supporting a community in Jinja, Uganda, called Together We Love Ministry, by chanting together with them and supporting their fundraising. They do not have access to vital resources such as regular sources of food, medical supplies and electricity, that we have at our fingertips every day. They rely on charity donations and crowdfunders to help them pay hospital bills and buy equipment such as mosquito nets and resources to build sustainable food solutions, as well as to send the children in their orphanage to school.

Being part of this project and seeing how this community manages to live with the bare minimum and still greet us with warm smiles when we come together on Zoom to chant is humbling. Fundraising with them has certainly been an eye opener, but it becomes all the more real and an affirmation of how fortunate I am when, for example, we are not able to connect with them because Masa Fredrick, one of their primary carers, does not have access to WiFi or money for data and cannot join the Zoom call. Masa explained to me that they feel very fortunate to now have a water supply flowing directly into their homes and that before this system was provided, they would have to walk for 5 hours to extract water from a borehole, carrying the water the 5 hour walk home. While the current situation is a huge improvement, they still have to make sure they are able to pay for the water they need every day, or they are not able to access the supply. When I think about switching on lights, household appliances and charging devices, I am now aware that Masa and his community still do not have electricity in their homes. They use candles to provide them with light when daylight fades, and these need to be bought daily from their local trade centre, a hour's walk away.

Can you imagine what it would be like to have to rely on candles every day so that when the sun went down you could do things like cook your dinner, have a shower, read a book, wash the dishes and charge your phone?

Can you imagine what it would be like if one day you did not have the money to buy the candles, or you were unable to walk to the trade centre?

We have probably all seen the heart-wrenching images in the charity adverts showing children walking for miles to get water that is not even fit to drink, but I hope that by sharing some of these personal, real life examples, and asking these questions, I will help my readers in developed countries to deepen their Gratitude practice, and that this will not only help to bring our neighbours in developing countries closer to our hearts, but to bring them to mind when we find ourselves in positions to be able to help them. I am deeply grateful to Masa for giving me permission to share this, and I hope that by bringing attention to his community, others will feel called to help in conscious and meaningful ways.

Essentially, instead of 'thinking of the starving children' as I remember hearing a lot in my youth, perhaps we can think of someone specific who doesn't have the same privileges as us. For me, it's my friend and ex-client SD and Masa. When we remember them, and how their focus every day is on their basic needs, it can remind us that most of our problems are relatively easy to solve and likely to be on the higher levels of the Hierarchy of Needs - this freedom is not available to everyone. Just as one example, Unicef reported that 2.2 billion people still do not have access to safely managed water supplies (Unicef, 2023). During one of the chanting sessions, Masa said something that really touched my heart. When asked how his community was doing, he said he was grateful that they were doing fine and put things inescapably into perspective, "Those who are breathing are succeeding."

You can connect with Masa and his community via their Instagram account @togetherweloveministry.

After 7 years of providing food for the homeless with my fantastic crew of 'Sandwich Ninjas' at Club Sandwich, the idea that we were providing for people who were themselves unable to meet their most basic need ignited some new thinking in me. While we made the sandwiches, there would be occasional challenges such as running out of bread or butter, but we would always have the resources to get more. We occasionally struggled with how to make a delicious nutritious snack that would be a whole meal for someone from ingredients that didn't necessarily complement each other. At one point it dawned on me that these were 'problems' that our homeless friends would love to have - they were stuck on the bottom level of the hierarchy where they needed to actively seek out food, water, clothing and shelter. This meant that they were unable to even reach their Safety Needs on the second level: personal security, property and more.

It was this thinking that led to the phrase:

Your Floor Could Be Someone's Ceiling.

Now I understood why it upset me so much seeing people on the street - their challenges are life and death ones every day, whereas mine are mainly in the top three levels. I have the privilege of pursuing my dreams and fulfilling my potential, and I felt a deep sense of injustice about this inequality.

And so, the lyrics to "Make It Right - The Gratitude Song" were born.

As incredibly good fortune would have it, I happened to be working in the same school as a wonderfully musical and talented lady, Geri O'Regan, who has become one of my closest friends. Our paths initially crossed when a colleague connected us, suggesting that we perform together at the school talent show. To say that we clicked is an understatement, and no sooner had I written the words, than Geri had come up with a beautiful melody, using 'only the good notes' at my request!

Scan the QR code below to hear
"Make It Right - The Gratitude Song"©
by Sarit Gafan and Geri O'Regan on YouTube.

Music: Geri O'Regan & Sarit Gafan

Lyrics: Sarit Gafan & Geri O'Regan

When the rain pours down and your smile turns upside down

The world feels like it's getting on your case

Just think, while you're screaming, someone could be dreaming

Of one day being in your place

Your first world situation could be someone's aspiration

To have a home, to keep them warm and dry

Someone else's biggest need, could be a family to feed

A job to break their cycle, so remember…

Your floor could be someone's ceiling

Your pain could be their healing

Your low could be someone's high

All we need is to unite

And make it right

When technology breaks down, help is nowhere to be found

How'd you feel when everything turns out OK?

Let me tell you I can see, there are people on the street

Need help to live life every single day

So my friends I think that now, is the time to make a vow

To focus on our blessings and gifts

The truth is giving back

Keeps your happiness on track

The more hands join, the more we can uplift

Your floor could be someone's ceiling

Your pain could be their healing

Your low could be someone's high

All we need is to unite

And make it right

Is getting wet really a threat?
Got a roof, ain't that the truth
Is buffering really suffering
Got more time to sit and rhyme!
Your floor could be someone's ceiling
Your pain could be their healing
Your low could be someone's high
All we need is to unite
And make it right

"Make it right" reflects my feeling that we can all do something to repair the imbalance and make the world right. It shouldn't just be some people who have the opportunity to fulfil their dreams, everyone should.

Our hope for the song was twofold:

To help people appreciate which of their higher needs are being met so that when things in their life feel difficult, they can be supported by a perspective of Gratitude removing the focus from the frustration or inconvenience.

To actually help people meet some of their basic needs, which is why we did some fundraising for homeless charities through launching the song.

Kindful Reader Reflections:

I invite you to take a look at Maslow's Hierarchy of Needs and reflect on which of your needs are being met today and on an average day. You can write in the space below or record your reflections in any way that feels right for you.

You could also create a colour coded 'Needs Check-In' Chart© for yourself like my one below if you wish. It is modelled on Maslow's Hierarchy of Needs and serves as a way to kindfully do a check in to see how you feel your needs are being met. You can either go through each level and place the relevant 'need' (e.g Food, Resources, Friendship etc) wherever you feel it sits, or just look at them all and see if any stand out as being clearly met or not met.

This is a somewhat simplistic technique but it gives you a quick temperature check as to whether you feel your needs are being met. If you place all the 'needs' on the chart, it can give you an overview as well as a more detailed idea of how you feel your needs are being met. For example, if most of your 'needs' are on the left, towards the happy face, you feel that most of your needs are being met and it may feel easier to feel grateful for them. If most are towards the right (the sad face), this can help you see which needs you are struggling with. I have found that food, water, air and shelter have been constant, and seeing them in that position on the board can really help when other needs are in jeopardy.

Gratitude Goldmine

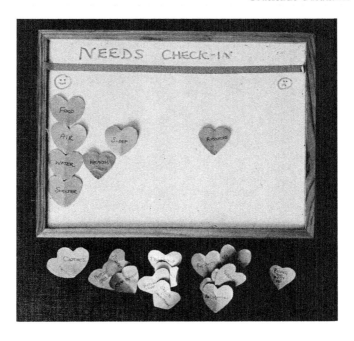

Needs Check-In Chart© Sarit Gafan, Highest Good Wellbeing, 2023

Chapter

6

Your Journey with Gratitude

While there may be a lot of evidence for what works in certain contexts and situations, I'm a big advocate of following what feels right for you. I invite you to let go of what you think might be 'the right way' and instead follow your heart. It's also important to start with being grateful for things that come easily to you. For example if you're very healthy or if you're happy with your living space or work situation, you could start with appreciating the gifts that they bring you. You could check through the Hierarchy of Needs and see which of your needs seem to be constantly and reliably met. Then when you are more practised and more confident, you could start to dig a little deeper into your Gratitude Goldmine to see if there are areas that are not so easy, but you can still find things to be grateful for around them. That's where the real gold is, because with regular practice on those areas, you could find that your energy improves around them. For example, money has been a challenge for me since I've been working part time. As I've become more aware of the choices I have, for example, the clothes in my wardrobe, the food and drink available to me, I find it easier to be more positive about my money situation.

Go at your own pace, practice at your own level and find the most nourishing ways for you to enjoy Gratitude and let it uplift your life, in whichever ways you want it to. No-one can tell you what you 'should' be grateful for, they're not walking in your shoes, fighting your battles or navigating your waters. I've found that, in time, the most meaningful practice can come from natural thought, responses and curiosity.

If you're suffering in any way, or if you're in a place of scarcity, my heart goes out to you. This book is a distilled vessel of my learnings, ideas, thoughts and practices, with the invitation to the reader to take what serves and leave anything that doesn't. I am well aware that we may all be in the same ocean of being human, but we are not all in the same boat. We all have a set of circumstances that is unique to us, and one thing that someone may find easy to deal with, may be the bane of another person's life – it is for no-one but you to judge how hard or easy your experience of life feels to you.

There may be times when you experience intense struggle and Gratitude may be the last thing on your mind - it may feel inaccessible, and that's OK. The important thing is to decide what role you would like it to play in your life, learn when it works for you, and to be aware of judging yourself if you're not able to feel grateful for something that seems obvious. Let me give you an example…

On a good day, it's easy to feel grateful for a job or pay cheque, but there might be days when work is stressful or the bills are piling up, and the idea of immersing yourself in thoughts about how lucky you are to even have a job just create toxic thoughts and emotions such as "How can I feel grateful for my job, it's so stressful!" or "How can I feel grateful for the money I receive? It just goes straight back out of my account!". In situations like these, it can be helpful to take a step back and first be kind to yourself. The point of this journey with Gratitude is to find ways for it to improve your life and for that good energy to radiate out into the world. Here are a couple of kind ways you could approach thought processes like these using Gratitude Practice:

1) First, acknowledge that you're experiencing some struggle and give yourself a mental hug for noticing it and experiencing it

2) Remind yourself that on a good day, you've noticed that Gratitude practice changes your energy from the inside and see if you can give it a try now

3) Then ask yourself this: What do I **feel able** to be grateful for in this moment?

You could also try some Self-Gratitude:

What am I grateful for about myself that has enabled me to get this far in life, or even just today?

Then acknowledge the challenges and meet them with the kind energy of gratitude:

It's true, work is feeling stressful, but can I be grateful for the fact that I got myself this job? Can I be grateful that I got myself into work this morning? Can I be grateful that I always do my best even when the going gets tough?

I don't want to make any assumptions about what life is like for you. I would like to try and meet you where you are, even if I don't have the opportunity to actually meet you. I don't know if you have all the use of your limbs or senses or have healthy systems and organs. It's important to take this journey at your own level – do what nourishes you, what has a positive effect on your energy.

Invited Practice:

Try exploring the different parts of you and the gifts they bring. For example, my feet enable me to stand up, what gifts does that bring? Once I'm standing up, what can I do?

You could record it as a list or a flowchart:

Standing up enables me to:

Get up in the morning without help

Take my place in a queue

Talk to others at eye level

Take myself places

Connect with the earth

Move

Keep Fit

Walk in nature

What does each of these then enable?

Kindful Reader Reflection: Did you notice any changes in your thinking while exploring this practice? You can note them here if you like:

I invite you to bring Gratitude into your awareness in ways that are meaningful, uplifting and nourishing, and practical for you, fitting in with your lifestyle and adding value to it. If, however, you're looking for something of an overhaul, I invite you to immerse yourself and see how it can actually make positive changes in your life. For example, you might look at the three benefits in the introduction, and see which resonates the most in this given moment, then as you read the book, highlight the concepts and practices that stand out as serving that goal. Each week you could add another practice, or each month if you need more time to embed the habit – go at your own pace and please be kind to yourself if you miss practices. This is about nourishing yourself and your world, and I guarantee you that beating yourself up is not anywhere in that equation!

I'm a firm believer of exploring the world, seeking out what nourishes me and then applying it in my own way, getting creative and playful with it. Gratitude Games can be a fun way to welcome this into your life and create more opportunities to practise naturally, whether you live alone, with family or others.

Gratitude A to Z is a really simple and playful game – you can print off a sheet of paper with the Alphabet on it, with a space next to each letter and stick it on the fridge or somewhere else prominent, and set yourself (and whoever you may live with) a goal of completing it within a set period of time, listing things that you're grateful for beginning with each letter of the alphabet. Then once it's full, show it to a friend, or look at it over dinner together.

One of my favourite games I created for my wellbeing workshops is Gratitude Awards. Each person pretends that they are accepting an award just for being themselves (why not!) and gives a speech thanking whoever and whatever they would like to. For example, "I would like to thank my Mum for encouraging me to broaden my horizons, the bus and driver for bringing me here and my body for enabling me to participate in this workshop."

Another one is Gratitude Eye Spy: "I spy with my grateful heart, something beginning with....M" You can then take turns to guess what it is that has been spied with that person's grateful heart and begins with M!

As with everything, please only play these when you can give them your full attention and keep yourself and others safe when playing them, especially if you're travelling on public transport for example.

I also invite you to explore ways to sprinkle Gratitude over your day in ways that naturally fit in with your life. For example, if you're not in a rush to unpack your shopping, make a mindful experience out of it by noticing how you feel about each item you unpack, and the goodness it will bring. For me, being able to afford shopping is a privilege, especially being able to afford to buy the food and products that I choose, rather than ones that I can afford, so taking a little time to appreciate them as they come into my daily life has opened me up to a greater sense of abundance.

You could take it one step further and appreciate the gifts that these items will bring you. You could ask yourself, "What is possible because I have these things?".

For example, I truly appreciate all the fresh food I can afford as it helps my body feel healthy and more natural.

Some Kind Reminders

Learn to be conscious and kindful in your practice - as it becomes more of a habit, try to make sure that you are maintaining ones that feel nourishing and letting go of those that do not. If it feels forced or like you're just going through the motions, like it's not coming from the heart, then it may not be purely Gratitude that you're practising! For example, you may be subconsciously trying to appease some guilt. In time, you can start to notice how pure Gratitude feels in your heart, in your mind and in your body, and if you're able to cultivate self-awareness, you'll be able to notice the value of your practice, and make any adjustments you need to get the best, most personalised experience for you.

One way to develop your self-awareness is through kindful practice of Gratitude. Instead of just jumping straight into it, you could set intentions for your practice by asking mindful questions:

What am I about to do? Why am I doing it?

Then when you finish:

How was this practice for me? Did I fulfil my intention? Do I feel nourished?

With this kindful approach you can notice if your mind wanders away from the intention, and gently and kindly guide it back.

The best way for you to practise and use Gratitude for physical and mental wellbeing depends on:

1) Where you feel you are on the Hierarchy of Needs
2) Where you are on a scale of wellbeing (remember, you can use the Self-Care Check In practice)
3) How much time you're able to commit to it
4) Your Self-Awareness

Balance is Key

We all lead busy lives, so it's vital that if you're doing this to improve your enjoyment of life, you find ways to make it enjoyable. This could mean choosing some light and short practices that feature regularly in your routine, with some deeper, less frequent ones for when you are able to allocate more time for them, perhaps once a week, or twice a month.

What's in your Gratitude Goldmine?

Everyone's is different, although of course there will be some common themes. It may also change all the time, depending on how you feel, where you go, what you do, who you're with etc. But one thing remains constant – YOU, and your response to what's happening in your life – that is where your power lies. So why not train yourself to guide your mind in a direction that feels better, and helps you stay level headed when the going gets tough, and you might find that sometimes tough isn't actually so tough.

At the end of the day, living life in this way is about purposefully training your brain, encouraging a positive perspective and actively seeking out what's going right for you – these are your Gratitude glasses! But they're not rose-tinted glasses, I like to think of them as ***reality magnifying glasses***! Enjoy!

Kindful Reader Reflections:

So, my friend, what have you learnt from the book so far that you feel you would like to experiment with?

Would you like to set yourself a tiny, fun goal to start incorporating Gratitude theory or practice into your life? In what ways? Perhaps you could look back through the earlier Kindful Reader Reflections for inspiration.

Chapter 7

My Journey with Gratitude: 14 Day Challenge Invitation

"All I knew was that a good energy had come to me and to my family, and now that I had benefited from it, I wanted to pass it on."

Day 1

Gratitude first came into my life in 2009 after several mental health breakthroughs and various family health-related wake up calls. It led me along a much happier path where I left the corporate world to pursue my dream of teaching and finally opened my heart to a romantic relationship after years of being closed. There was an initial feeling of relief for the wake up calls being misses and not hits, and for the restoration of my mental health and wellbeing after years of depression. As the reality of the storms that had now passed hit me, the relief gave way to a deep sense of Gratitude – I was so grateful to feel myself again, to feel part of the world again and to feel valuable again.

The feeling of Gratitude transformed into a deep desire to help other people who were suffering. I felt compelled to do something meaningful and concrete, to keep this vibration alive and spreading outwards to others. It is only through writing this book, that I now realise that I initially did not feel grateful towards a particular person, in fact, I could not define or pinpoint who or what I felt was responsible for my good fortune. This was the tip of my spiritual iceberg, only I didn't yet know it!

Kindful Reader Reflections:

Have you ever had a 'near miss' or a 'wake-up call'?

Do you feel it changed you or your outlook in any way?

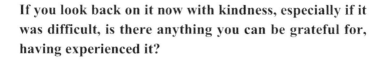

If you look back on it now with kindness, especially if it was difficult, is there anything you can be grateful for, having experienced it?

Invited Practice: Choose a creative way to record any silver linings (or 'golden reflections'!) that spring to mind. See the Pool of Practices chapter for some ideas.

Day 2

With the exception of the excellent medical professionals who were involved in healing my family, I could not fathom how or why we had had such lucky escapes, nor did I fully grasp how I had managed to break out of the depression. But I did believe that a good energy had come to us; a kind energy that had helped my family and I, and now that I had benefited from it, I was eager to pass it on.

Inspiration came clearly and swiftly. I discovered that my beloved late Grandmother was making sandwiches for the homeless, and my creative mind daydreamed of a club where friends gathered to do this together, with music playing and conversations flowing, so that many hearts would make happy work of feeding more people.

And so Club Sandwich was born!

It started as a small group of friends getting together once a month to make sandwiches for the homeless people served by New Hope, a Watford based charity. What I loved about it, was that everyone contributed at their own level, what they could afford; loaves of bread, fillings and spreads, and with support and donations from family, friends and supportive business owners, it began to flourish into a larger operation.

It made my heart sing and I was inspired by the notion that many smaller contributions (not just the ingredients, but time, energy, love, equipment and even transport) could produce mountains of food for hungry people, and I believe it was this energy and intention that attracted groups of 15-

20 people or more at times to make up around 200 sandwiches. The energy in the club was wonderfully uplifting; people were so focused on getting the job done, and done well, that for the few hours we were together it almost felt like we were on a different planet – a planet where life problems didn't exist! The only problems we encountered during that time were either running out of margarine or the dilemma of whether or not our homeless friends would enjoy a combination of hummus and coleslaw!

Kindful Reader Reflections:

Have you ever been involved in helping in some way and found that you forgot about your own struggle?

How did it feel to be able to help?

How did it feel to dip your toe into a world where people needed help, and to then return to your own world where you yourself did not need that help?

Invited Practice: Reflect on things that you have needed help with, and whether or not you were able to receive the help you needed, how and where it came from. Record this however you wish, being creative if that feels nourishing. Does this practice open up new avenues of Gratitude for you?

Day 3

Witnessing people who were so engaged in something so selflessly and with such care was a real honour.

It was a space free from ego.

Naturally, there was the occasional misplaced comment about knotting sandwich bags without getting all the air out (guilty!) or overzealous spreading, **but we all knew that was because it wasn't just marmite we were spreading.**

It was love.

And you just can't spread love too thickly, especially for people who are struggling to survive each day. And so the motto, "Spread the Love" came alive!

The club continued for several years, with the dedication of some close friends helping me to manage it and maintain the standard of service with the growing numbers. Meanwhile, the pangs of sadness for those who were struggling to have even their most basic of needs met became stronger and I wanted to do more. Sandwiches were no longer enough. I wanted to at least offer something that would stay with our homeless friends longer than the time it took to digest it. I made some enquiries of our partner charity, and we ran several seasonal provision-focused projects, including Blankets and Blessings and Shoebox Shenanigans.

The difference was not just in what we were providing (blankets, shoeboxes filled with toiletries, underwear and more), but we were now also sending heartfelt notes and cards. This had been inspired by my experiences of Tony Robbins' Basket Brigade scheme – every Christmas, groups of people gather to pack and deliver thousands of donated Christmas meals to families in need. I noticed that volunteers were sitting at tables writing cards, and these were not simply, "Merry Christmas", they were unhurried, sincere and detailed good wishes for a better life. "Yes!" I thought, "Until I can physically do more to help, that's a great way to spread more love." Upon receiving our first round of cards, I was told by one of the managers of a new shelter we were serving, that there was 'not a dry eye in the house'. I hoped that they were tears of hope and comfort at feeling cared for, and that we had succeeded in helping our homeless friends to at least feel loved and not forgotten, even though we couldn't provide them with their most basic of needs – a home.

Kindful Reader Reflections:

Take another look at the figure of Maslow's Hierarchy of Needs – can you think of a time when any of your basic needs have not been met?

Gratitude Goldmine

I invite you to reflect with kindness about any help you may have received or any action you were able to take yourself to resolve this.

Looking back at this situation, is there anything you feel able to be grateful for?

Invited Practice: Take a tour of your home, mindfully taking inventory of each room, asking,

What/Who helps me in my life?

What could I not manage without?

As you go round each room, list or record in your own way one or two of the gifts you notice, for example, in the kitchen you may notice the sink and how there is always clean water to drink and warm water to wash up with. You could display the list in each room and add more as you notice them. You could also expand this exercise into a mind map or other representation of the gifts that are present in each room of your home to get a bigger picture of how it all comes together to help keep your life flowing. Keeping these visual representations visible is a good way to develop your awareness of other things you can be grateful for, as well as being a positive prompt if you're feeling a little low.

A kind reminder here though, if you're feeling really low, please be kind to yourself.

Day 4

In 2013, I had been in my new teaching career for 6 years, but was still struggling to feel self-actualised. As a result, waves of negative thoughts were rising again and I wasn't feeling my awesome self. My sister had recommended a course called The Phil Parker Lightning Process® (LP) and supported me to do it myself. It was in doing this course that I first encountered the Negativity Bias, and it blew my mind. It was such a relief to understand why I'd been subconsciously bombarding myself with negative thoughts, and to have at least a partial, even scientific explanation as to why life was feeling so hard again. The first time round it had been a series of traumatic experiences, combined with my sensitivity, lack of self-acceptance or coping strategies and a destructive web of limiting beliefs. Yep, that'll do it!

Armed with this new knowledge, I began learning to rewire my brain to focus on what I wanted in any given situation. The course was very powerful, and for some time I used it to bring up my level of wellbeing enough to feel myself again, and steer myself onto a better path.

This rewiring was pivotal and laid the foundation to my journey into healthier mental wellbeing. I trained my brain so that I became more aware of my thoughts, and was able to create a strong, kind buffer - an intervening reminder that I can always choose my thoughts and therefore how I respond. I found the Lightning Process particularly powerful because it also involved the use of my imagination to visualise positive outcomes in inspiring and creative ways, and my brain just loves doing that!

This self-awareness was the first step in improving my mental wellbeing through Gratitude – it cleared a mental path for me and left a space to start consciously choosing what to place my focus on, starting with what I'm grateful for!

Kindful Reader Reflections:

What have you learned in your life that has changed it for the better?

My purposeful learning led to positive change in my life. Can you think of anything that you have learnt on purpose that has improved your life? Perhaps it was a new habit, a skill or something learned through a course. How did it improve your life?

Can you think of anything you have naturally learnt from *life* that has changed *your life* for the better?

Invited Practice:

Set the intention to start noticing your learning and the gifts it has brought you, and may continue to bring you. For example, what have you learnt about your work? How does it help you enjoy it? Or what about your life? What do you now know about your own life that you didn't know years ago that has enabled you to live a better one?

If you feel called to, record this in a personalised way that is meaningful to you.

Day 5

With the new energy that the Lightning Process brought me, I was so grateful to be able to bring people together once a month for the privilege of serving the homeless. After a while, though, I started to feel a change in my energy. Looking back, this coincided with the beginning of my spiritual awakening, but it was no coincidence!

It was now 2015, and after attending a spiritual meditation event with Illa and Jeetu Khagram of Radiant Lotus, I finally had the awakening that made me realise that I was not imagining the voice inside me whispering, "You are here for a reason." I had been hearing this voice since the age of 15, when I was washing up and a cup on the rack had fallen on its side. The voice told me, "Pick up the fallen." At the time, I was already in quite a dark place, so I was unable to hear the divine message behind this voice. I thought there was something wrong with me, or that I was actually going mad.

Little did I know that it was not fallen cups that I was being guided to help, but fallen people…

…and I would have to start with myself.

As I attended more events and began to learn to meditate and 'drown out the noise', I was hearing my inner voice more clearly. On one occasion, I saw how my Meditation teachers offered Gratitude for their food, and something clicked into place:

"This is how you stop taking things for granted."

I remembered how at the primary school I went to, we would say Grace After Meals after every lunch, and how we would all dutifully sing every word by rote. I remembered thinking that I didn't really understand it all, and that I was more focused on getting the words right than the sentiment. The way that my teachers did their Gratitude practice was different. They put their hands on either side of their plates, took a deep breath in to slow down and be fully present with their meal, and then said a short prayer to say thank you to the earth and their own representation of a Divine Source.

I found myself developing this practice in my own way, depending on my mood and the time I had available. If I was able to flow at a mindful and leisurely pace, I would start going through the processes it took for my food and drink to arrive in front of me. It felt nourishing and awe-inspiring to pay attention to the farmers who had planted the vegetables, the earth that had provided the nutrients to grow the food, the plants that had worked in harmony with nature to produce such nourishment for us humans, the people who had picked and prepared them – it was not just mind blowing but heart-blowing! Having learnt the importance of practising authentically and flexibly, and not to force them, I would sometimes just think of one new thing to be grateful for that I had never thought about, for example, my cutlery, the table legs, the origins of these things – mother earth providing the metal from her core and the trees that provided the wood, or the people who designed the furniture I was using. As I wrote this section, I realised that this practice also highlighted to me the individual impact of my life on this planet. I am grateful for this awareness too and how it will empower me to minimise my negative impact on our beautiful Earth.

Kindful Reader Reflections:

Take a moment to think of the last meal you had. How does it feel to be aware of the people, things, systems and processes involved in providing your food and drink?

Invited Practice: Create an Honour Roll of all the people and things that enable you to have one meal. Do this in the way that speaks to you the most from the options in the Pool of Practices chapter, or choose your own way.

Day 6

With this new energy shaking up my belief systems, I had begun to question the value of what we were doing at Club Sandwich. It was wonderful to know that people were coming together to serve others, but I couldn't stop thinking that after they finished eating the sandwiches, our homeless friends' lives had essentially not improved much.

They were still homeless.

With no immediate inspiration about how to make our efforts more sustainable, I began by striving to make them more conscious. I introduced light practices into the sandwich making sessions, and eventually ran events with other groups that revolved around gratitude – I thought of it as conscious volunteering. We would brainstorm encouraging messages we could send along with the food, being mindful of our phrasing, and trying to put ourselves in the shoes of our recipients.

If I was homeless and receiving a message from a stranger, what would I want to hear?

People seemed more fulfilled by this kind of volunteering as they connected more deeply with the intention and energy behind their giving. It gave them the opportunity to take a mindful pause and appreciate that this wasn't just a fun social with a purpose, it was the practice of not taking the provision of our basic needs for granted, and paying forward their gratitude for being free to enjoy so much of what this world has to offer.

By November 2015, I had started noticing homeless people and their world more and more, with a deep sadness and frustration. I found myself unable to walk by without at least talking with them and trying to give them something they needed, even if it was just a few warm words – it felt completely unjust and unthinkable that people should have to live in public spaces, without the safety and security of four walls and ceiling, and a door to close to the dangers and disturbances of the outside world.

In my work as an educator, I was noticing things too. Whenever we had a fire drill and had to assemble outside while leaving behind our belongings, the kids would have a drill of their own.

"What about my stuff?"

I loved working with them, and knew that they were still young to be thinking beyond their immediate needs, but I felt a pang of frustration. I had also felt a sadness that the world has an unbalanced focus on the material, and that this was hindering humanity's potential for evolving into a race of tuned-in individuals supporting each other and the planet to be the best versions of themselves. I felt that if we could teach children at an early age to appreciate the things that need to be in place in order for them to meet their higher needs, they could grow up with more resilience to inevitable ups and downs of life, and flow with them rather than be upended by them. I realised that, as Gandhi said, I would need to "Be the change I wish to see in the world".

Kindful Reader Reflections:

Can you think of anything in your life that is not material or tangible that brings you gifts? Things that you can't touch or hold, but make your life better?

If you're struggling to think of something, walk yourself through your day, noticing times when:

- You know how to do things
- You're able to do things independently
- You feel good/nourished/confident

Ask yourself, "How is this possible?"

How does it feel to become more aware of these gifts?

Invited practice:

In your own way, create a representation of these gifts, or how you feel about them.

Day 7

Feeling more aware of the world of the homeless, I was noticing things in my own world too. How easy it was to get frustrated when the internet was slow, transport delays kept me waiting in cold or wet weather or my washing machine broke down. I remembered Club Sandwich and the fact that I was someone who had the privilege of being able to provide for others, which meant that I didn't need help with my own basic needs. If my internet was slow, it just meant that I had some time to ponder or organise myself while it recalibrated, but it would always come through for me and meet my needs. If transport delays meant being cold or getting wet, it was no big deal, I could easily get a change of clothes or dry off, and even warm up in a hot shower if necessary, and being late was not the end of the world – my world was not going anywhere. When my washing machine broke down, I had the option of taking my laundry to the laundrette, or if necessary my kind neighbours offered to let it hitch a ride in theirs! None of this was earth shattering for me – everything was taken care of, even when things went 'wrong'. In fact, I felt that these were 'First World' privileges for me*. I was developing a deeper, more practical understanding of how fortunate I am, and the question
"Is buffering really suffering?"

ignited the idea for the lyrics of "Make It Right – The Gratitude Song".

My dear and very talented friend and now singing partner, Geri O'Regan, waved her musical wand over them, and together we created a charity song to raise money for several homeless charities. It focused on the notion that "Your floor could be someone's ceiling, your pain could be their healing" – what you see as a really bad day, could be the best-case scenario for someone experiencing life differently.

* At this point, I would like to acknowledge with kindness that not everyone reading this will have the same privileges I am grateful for and fortunate enough to have, and it may be that some of you may not even have some of your basic needs met. I am sharing my own experiences and I would never expect anyone who does not feel that their needs are met to talk themselves into that, or feel obliged to feel grateful for what they have. My invitation is to look at the Hierarchy of Needs, and see where you are on it, then see if there is anything you feel can help you access Gratitude through this practice. If not, please just offer yourself kindness, take good care of yourself and I hope that you get the help that you need to move yourself up.

Kindful Reader Reflections:

Take a look at the lyrics to Make It Right - The Gratitude Song, or have a listen to it.

Looking back, are there any situations in the song that you can relate to or have had similar experiences?

Did buffering feel like suffering? Have you really needed the internet to be working under time pressure but it just wasn't?

Was getting wet a threat? Did you get caught in rough weather and feel stressed or frustrated?

When things were resolved, were you able to feel grateful that these were only temporary experiences?

Invited practice:

Can you think of any situations where technology broke down or things did not work, resulting in a stressful experience? With kindness, visualise the situation when it was resolved or after enough time had passed that it was no longer stressful.

Are you able to explore appreciation in your mind's eye, or in any way that feels nourishing, for:

- The solution?
- Whatever was not working, and what it does for you or helps you do when it works normally?
- The experience itself?

Day 8

The first charity we raised money for was The Passage, a London based charity whose motto of "Giving a hand up, not a hand out" resonated deeply with me. I had long felt that charity needed to take on a whole person approach and support people into independence rather than just put a plaster on a problem that would only recur. Their sustainable approach to getting people off the street to deal with the reasons for their situation through an ongoing programme inspired Geri and I to put our best musical foot forward through a JustGiving campaign to help The Passage break the cycle of homelessness for as many people as possible.

Having felt myself come alive in the running and growing of Club Sandwich, I followed my heart and left my job in education to find a full time charity job. My dream came true when I had the incredible opportunity of leading Light Up A Life, a winter volunteering project supporting charities during the Christmas period, when they may lose their regular volunteers. It was through working with many inspiring charities as part of this role that I discovered the second homeless charity that Geri and I wished to support through our Gratitude Song.

Rhythms of Life and its inspiringly stoic Founder, Andrew Faris, knocked me for six. Unlike The Passage, with its paid staff and corporate partnerships, Rhythms of Life runs purely on volunteer power and its partnerships with food retailers who want to ensure their surplus food is seen rightfully home to those who desperately need it. To top it all off, I got to know Andrew (or Faris as he's known to most) and discovered that he launched the charity after being homeless for 6 years. With his determined and enterprising nature, he managed to get himself off the street, but instead of building a life for himself he put all his energy into the charity. He wanted to make sure that the people he had left behind on the streets would not have to face the same difficulties that he had in trying to break the cycle. He once told me that, when he was experiencing homelessness, some charities had certain conditions they would place upon their beneficiaries and he did not want anyone to have to jump through hoops in order to have their basic needs met. The priority for him was to simply help people up from the bottom rung of the Hierarchy of Needs, not to influence them or get something in return. This is truly unconditional service, something I'm learning more and more about on my spiritual journey. It is human nature to expect people to be grateful when we help them, but that expectation itself places a judgement on the person if they are not able to feel Gratitude, and therefore a condition on the service.

Your own Kindful Reader Reflections and Practice:

For the next seven days of the challenge, I'm leaving this space open for your own reflections. This is a good way to engage more deeply and independently with Gratitude, but if nothing comes to mind, you can always take inspiration from the earlier reflections. Either way, I invite you to go with what comes into your heart.

Invited practice:

For the next seven days, I invite you to try out any of the practices in the Pool of Practices chapter, repeat earlier ones, or come up with your own. This supports the intention for you to follow your own path with Gratitude.

Day 9

Andrew Faris showed me a whole new level of paying Gratitude forward – this man had sacrificed the chance to make a life for himself to help others rebuild theirs. The charity became his life, and I was utterly blown away by his commitment and ability to run such a high impact service without regular funding or the resources available to other charities - he lets nothing stop his service. Since 2008 Rhythms of Life has been serving hot meals and offering provisions to thousands of homeless people on the streets of London 365 days a year, with no regular funding, and no permanent home.

It was a sad irony; this amazing charity that serves homeless people is homeless itself.

The only way they had managed to continue operating was by moving from place to place, with all their tonnes of donated resources, through Andrew's tireless work on building partnerships. This means that to this day, every day is a struggle to raise funds for their next base of operations. I felt utterly inspired by Andrew's selfless dedication and the clear impact it was having on so many people, but I was also saddened that it came at such a cost to his own life - like the charity, he too is living day to day with no fixed abode. With the intention of showing our gratitude to Andrew for his unconditional service, Geri and I re-recorded our song to raise funds for Rhythms of Life.

Your own Kindful Reader Reflections and Practice:

Day 10

While I had seen the cost of serving from an empty cup through Andrew's life and the circumstances of his charity, this sparked a new journey in my personal development. Through my work with a mentor, Tom C. Kelly, I realised that on a much smaller scale, I had been putting others first throughout my life. While clearly not to the same sacrificial extent as Andrew had, Tom helped me realise that the greatest gift I could give to others was to serve them from a full cup. This was opposed to the way I had been living, which was to run around and try to make everyone else happy, leading to several episodes of burnout. Initially, I dealt with this in a practical way, with Tom's suggestion of giving myself what I wanted for a while to see how it felt.

It was amazing! I started to feel 'fuller', more enriched, more energised (partly due to gifting myself the services of a personal trainer!) and more myself.

What I didn't realise was that I was now starting to include myself in the practice of Gratitude!

I can imagine that some alarms may be going off here, but we're not talking about self-congratulation or gratification from a place of ego. I see Self-Gratitude as a vital part of the wellbeing picture, as well as the spiritual picture - it is an act of self-love. While I believe that we are experiencing and receiving countless blessings and gifts all the time from external sources, without our active and willing (and sometimes unwilling!) participation and natural proclivity to do our best at all times, none of it would have much impact on our lives. As I said about the spiritual journey, I believe it's 50/50 - receive 50% and do your 50%, so I learnt that just as I thank the higher energies, it's also important to thank myself and appreciate all that I do to live my best possible life.

During this phase of self-development, I found the solution to my burgeoning desire to effect greater impact for people who were struggling by setting up my own mental wellbeing company, Highest Good Wellbeing. Having realised that I was only able to go for my dreams (self-actualisation on the highest level of the Hierarchy of Needs) once my mental wellbeing was stable, I realised that part of my purpose on this earth is to help people to move themselves up the hierarchy of needs.

Your own Kindful Reader Reflections and Practice:

Day 11

After a trip to Thailand in 2017, where I had a profound experience in one of the temples, meditation and Gratitude became a daily practice. I started to notice that Gratitude made me feel happy but also brought about a calmness and peace during practice, which rippled out into the other areas of my life. Eventually it became embedded in daily life, almost like a new lens through which to look at life. I noticed that, if I was more mindful of what I was doing when performing simple daily tasks like washing my face, cooking, eating, taking a shower,

I became aware of how so much is going right, all the time, without any effort from me, and this grounded me in a beautiful energy and in the present moment.

I had become fascinated and even amazed by these things and appreciated them as daily blessings and miracles that happened, whether I noticed them or not.

I decided that choosing to notice them was a nourishing way to live.

I started to research incredible facts that put things into perspective for me. For example, in order to be able to speak, around a hundred different muscles in the chest, neck, jaw, tongue, and lips must work together, and there are on average, approximately 30,000 parts needed to make a car. This helped me become more mindful about the things that were making my life seriously easy, and maintain balance through life's ups and down, like some of the 'First World problems' I mention in The Gratitude Song.

On returning from Thailand, I was now on a soul-searching break having left my career in schools to find my true purpose. I had felt frustrated at not being able to make enough of a difference within the education system and took a courageous leap of faith into nothingness to see if I could make a bigger difference outside of it. My 40th birthday was fast approaching, and I asked myself what I wanted to give myself for this milestone of my journey. I'd been dancing around my writing for years, and like many other writers, had reams of unpublished pieces whispering sweet nothings to each other in my cupboards. I decided to give myself the kindness of a fresh start and knew instantly that I wanted to write a Gratitude blog! But I found myself writing not just about Gratitude. What flowed forth was a kindful, retrospective look at the life lessons I'd been experiencing, through the eyes of Gratitude. I felt that I had learnt so much by reflecting on the challenges in my life, and was now able to see through this beautiful lens some of the incredible learning and blessings that had forged my unique path.

These were often things that were hard to accept at the time, but looking back, with kindness as always, I could see the gifts they had brought.

A shining example of this is that, most of my dating life I had sought out alpha males and was constantly getting hurt in such relationships. It wasn't until I did some inner work that I realised that this was the wrong kind of man for me –

he would have alpha'd all over me and my unconventional ways, and most likely not let be me. If I had not done this inner work, followed my inner guidance, my intuition, I would never have opened my heart to my wonderful fiancé, who balances and complements me with his unassuming, introverted nature, but is an absolute grounded tree trunk for me to freely spread my branches and fruit into the world! In the end, I am also grateful that we met at a silent dating party, because it provided the opportunity to be lit up by the warmth, fun and kindness in his smile, and to see the light in his eyes that showed me there was more to him than met…..mine! If we'd have been at a conventional party or event, I may have dismissed him as 'too quiet' – I'm grateful for my open-heart and open-mind that enabled me to follow my intuition!

Having learnt the importance of self-kindness and kindfulness for mental wellbeing, I started a Gratitude blog on my website with these in mind when reflecting on my experiences.

Your own Kindful Reader Reflections and Practice:

Day 12

In 2018, as the Universe teamed up with me to make another dream come true, I qualified as a Happiness Trainer with the Museum of Happiness. It was like coming home. Since breaking out of the depression, I had been longing to teach the soft skills I had come to cherish, but the Universe knew better – I had to fully learn the skills of self-awareness, self-kindness and self-nourishment before I could teach them to others. Until then, I had to make do with teaching English as a Second Language and pour my passion for the 'softness' into that. The Museum of Happiness course felt as though it validated the learning I had taken from my experiences; an affirmation that what I had gone through and what I had learnt from it served the purpose in the service of humanity I had been longing to provide. Among the treasures I found within the course content, I learnt that I was not alone in my mission to spread the message that we all deserve to be happy, and there are wonderfully fun, nourishing and science-backed ways to cultivate that energy in our lives, Gratitude practice being one of them!

As I discovered the wealth of scientific studies that had been proving the benefits of Gratitude practice, I finally felt that with some science behind the 'softness', there was nothing stopping from me from being unapologetically me, and serving my purpose on this earth:

To help people feel good!

Having stepped in as the Museum's Interim Community Co-ordinator during a transition period, I led talks, workshops and meditations on Gratitude, Self-Gratitude as an element of self-love and other Happiness topics, and went on to run my own mental wellbeing workshops. As I brought my unique take on Gratitude into their events and workshops, with the depth and sincerity I had embraced through my spiritual journey, it was awesome to learn from the team that balancing this with a lighter playful practice was truly nourishing. Gratitude Bingo was the first game I learnt on the course, and it was the same game that we shared with Russell Howard when he visited the Museum as part of his "Live Forever" segment.

It had the excitement that the game of bingo offered, but instead of being competitive, it was simply about playfully and creatively connecting and exploring what different people were grateful for.

As part of the course, I learnt about Mindfulness from expert, Shamash Alidina. It added a new layer, not only to my meditation practice, but to my Gratitude practice. The practice of slowing down, pausing, breathing and being present only with what is, lent itself beautifully to Gratitude practice. Firstly, Mindfulness gave me a buffer, between my thoughts and my reactions, which up until then were often judgements. Mindfulness built on the Self-Awareness I had begun to develop within myself, by creating a place of noticing. Over time, that place of noticing has become a space to choose. More and more I find that I have the space to choose responses rather than deal with reactions. Mindfulness provided a space in which to observe with kindness, and in that space, I became more grateful! As I became more mindful, I became more grateful as I noticed more of what was going right, without any conscious effort or attention from me.

I feel grateful in both general and specific ways:

I am grateful for the experience of doing the Happiness Train the Trainer course as it deeply affirmed my own learning and has empowered me to keep radiating that learning more and more.

I am grateful to Victoria Johnson, Shamash Alidina and all the team for creating the course and for making the Museum of Happiness a reality - a place for people to develop the most important skills in life in artistic, scientific and fun ways, and with such love and compassion.

Your own Kindful Reader Reflections and Practice:

Day 13

In September 2018, I wanted to do more with writing. I enjoyed the responses I received to my blog, and felt a calling to spread the Gratitude message further and wider. I also wanted to fulfil my dream of turning professional, after part of my charity job role involved me spotlighting amazing charities and writing about them. This small success gave me hope that I could find a company that believed in me enough to pay me to write for them. Knowing that my past job hunting attempts had proven stressful and fruitless, I took a new approach. I meditated.

I sat in silence and literally asked the Divine Source, "How can I become a professional writer?"

The answer came: "Soul and Spirit Magazine."

I was not yet aware of the publication, but it didn't take me long to realise that it was a great match for my spiritual values. I began emailing and calling, and over time developed a great relationship with the editor, Rosalind Moody. I soon realised I was playing a long game, but I meditated every step of the way, and eventually, I pitched my angle on Gratitude for the magazine, and Rosalind commissioned me to write my first professional article.

The article was published in December 2019 and was titled, "Master the Art of Giving Thanks". It offered a reflective ritual looking back on the year through the eyes of Gratitude. I went on to write two more articles, which are on my website with kind permission from Soul & Spirit Magazine.

Your own Kindful Reader Reflections and Practice:

Day 14

While Gratitude, for me, is a lifestyle choice, there is still a time and place for it. In March 2020, I came down with 'some kind of virus' with a cough that made it difficult to employ my favourite de-stressing breathing techniques. I didn't realise it at the time, I was on the bottom level of the pyramid of Maslow's Hierarchy of Needs, struggling to meet my most basic need - air. I wasn't able to feel grateful for much at that point, because I felt physically awful and had slipped into 'survival mode' without realising it. So despite all my experience, learning and training, the physical pain and discomfort, coupled with my inability to serve the world with my wellbeing know how at a time when people needed it the most, along with the fear of not knowing what my personal experience of the pandemic would be, triggered my stress response and sent me into a downward spiral, in other words, 'survival mode'. Fortunately, my self-awareness soon kicked in and I realised that I was not living my values - I was not treating myself with the same kindness I would offer to anyone else who was ill or experiencing struggle. I realised that I had been judging myself for being ill, which had led to incredibly unhelpful thoughts about me being useless!

I'm so grateful for this self-awareness flagging up this destructive experience. When I saw how low I was, I realised that I could not lift myself up without the help of some higher energy. I prayed and meditated and received guidance to create a new technique - the Self-Care Check In. It enabled me to regularly tune in to how I was feeling, physically and mentally, and to notice any connections between the two. When I tried this technique and found myself to be on the very bottom of the scale, I felt guided to put myself in 'Self-Care Mode', with an alarm every hour to prompt me to repeat the Self-Care Check In and continue to monitor how I was feeling physically and mentally and to apply self-kindness to move myself up the scale one point at a time. Later on, when I was feeling emotionally safer, in other words, more stable and able to cope with my situation, I was able to access my Gratitude practice and keep moving myself up the scale until I felt well enough to step back into my world!

I am incredibly grateful for receiving this technique, as it has enabled me to kindfully navigate some very difficult and stressful periods in my life.

As I write this now, in the summer of 2024, my most recent learning about Gratitude practice is that it can act as a great 'emotional temperature check'. If I notice that I'm not 'feeling it' when I practise, I check in with myself and find that my energy is low or there are some uncomfortable emotions swimming around. That was the case when I had the virus, but at that point, my being physically ill led to stress, which caused depleted emotional resilience and self-awareness. My usual strategies were inhibited by the stress, so the old unhelpful 'strategies' kicked in subconsciously – self-judgement and feeling like a victim. So when I tried to feel grateful for something but couldn't because I felt ill, I felt guilty. The me of now, however, would have said to my virus-stricken self:

"Hey, it looks like you're really struggling with this. It's more important for you to be kind to yourself right now, get better and not worry about being a good human being and trying to help others. Being a good human to **yourself** is what's important right now, so what do you need to feel better?"

In fact, the Sarit of today recognises that part of being a 'good' human being is that while 'me me me' is a selfish attitude, 'me first', in balance of course, is essential for a happy life.

I believe we are here to thrive and help others thrive, but that they don't need to come at a cost to one another if we invest in our wellbeing regularly.

You cannot serve from an empty cup.

The me of now has come to recognise that Gratitude is a nourishing and empowering attitude, and its practice is key for filling my cup with good energy. Attuning my focus to what's going right, and remembering that for fortunate people like me, most of the time, most things ARE going right, helps me live in a Positivity Bias, no matter what is going on around me. It means actively digging into my own personal Gratitude Goldmine, spending time there to continuously explore its treasures.

While I don't practise everything I've shared in this book every day, Gratitude has become a beautiful layer of goodness in my life, a treasured resource in my mental wellbeing toolkit. It is the last thing I do before I sleep and the first thing I do when I wake up, so if I find that I'm struggling with it, and not naturally feeling grateful, I know that I need to check in with myself.

As a wellbeing maintenance tool, I learnt that in order to gain the most benefit from Gratitude practice, I need to treat it like a muscle. I do this by 'exercising' it through regular touch points throughout the day, such as actively seeking out what I feel grateful for before bed and upon waking, and just before eating or drinking. These have become nourishing habits, while creative techniques, such as having a Gratitude Trellis and Maslow's Hierarchy board in my home and heart-shaped box with Gratitude heart notes are visual prompts for the in between times. Having them visible and available makes them a natural part of my lifestyle and I find that they catch my eye and gently beckon engagement.

Maintaining my day to day practice enables me to notice when I don't feel grateful and need to take care of myself and has created a mindset that supports me during difficult times, along with the rest of my mental wellbeing toolkit and spiritual practices.

Sarit Gafan

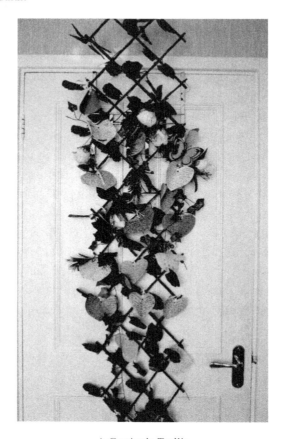

A Gratitude Trellis

Your own Kindful Reader
Reflections and Practice:

What strategies do you feel will work for you? Note down some ideas and allow for this to take time, experimentation and continuous evolution.

Chapter

8

Heartful Conclusions

I believe that the true meaning and purpose of practising Gratitude is genuinely appreciating what you have, all around you and within you, and the exponential gifts that emanate from everything that is going right, and everything that you already have. It's about taking a deep breath and extending your roots of love out into your world, and seeking out the goodness, the light, the help, the support from everything and everyone, and then **bless it with your thanks**.

To me, a Gratitude mindset means enjoying what you have and looking for things to appreciate in whatever comes to you, even if it means finding ways to dig a little deeper. This is as opposed to the consumerist mindset of societies in the developed world. We seem to be constantly seeking out more and more; more 'things and stuff', more technology, new things to decorate our homes and lives with, and we rarely pause to appreciate them, so we never feel truly satisfied.

I therefore feel that a Gratitude mindset can be good for the planet, as well as its inhabitants. Developing a mindset where we appreciate and are content with what is in front of us more, such as our existing provisions, resources and opportunities, we could learn to reduce our consumption. I am not just talking about switching off devices to go and connect with nature, although that could be a great start. Just as an example, since connecting with Masa and his community on a personal level, I have become more aware of food waste and take more care to prevent it in my home and beyond.

If you're struggling with scarcity in your life, as many of us do at varying levels, once again, my heart goes out to you. I don't see Gratitude as a 'making do with what you've got' mind set, but more of a look closely and heartfully about how what you have can serve you – it's a concept of resources. A recent example I can offer is, during the start up phase of my mental wellbeing company, I have had to become very good at budgeting.

One day I stained my favourite jumper, and in preparing to go out, I thought I didn't have anything else that was warm enough to wear but not too bulky to fit under my thick winter coat. I had another look through my wardrobe, and it was true, most of my clothes were light layers, that even combined would not have worked or felt comfortable. But then hope called to me, in the form of my pink light knitted jumper – I had overlooked it because of its design, but when I tried it on I realised it actually did the job perfectly. In that moment I was so thankful that:

1) I had something in my possession already that solved my problem

2) I didn't have to think about spending more money

3) I had the openness and mindfulness to be more present with my existing resources and make the most of them.

It was a very satisfying moment, and it helped me:

- Defuse the potential 'I don't have anything to wear' stress and the ensuing thoughts of scarcity and lack

- Feel responsible and strong for not needing to exceed my budget!

My wellbeing work has helped me to accept that I am not perfect and I cannot control life's ups and downs. There may well be times when I cannot feel grateful because I am too far down the wellbeing scale and only self-kindness will help. I have discovered the best use of Gratitude for in the moment mental wellbeing rescue for me. Everyone's scale of how they feel is relative to their unique perception and experience, but what I found was that if I check in with myself (a regular feature of my mental wellbeing maintenance) and find that I'm only struggling a little, say 6/10 or thereabouts, Gratitude practice is a great bridging strategy to move me up the scale one point at a time. The more you work with Gratitude on your own terms, the more you'll find the gold standard for yourself, your own Gratitude Goldmine.

Reflecting in retrospect through the eyes of Gratitude has been a powerful aspect of my practice. For example, I can be grateful for the challenges that led me into depression and helped me awaken from it, otherwise I wouldn't have improved my enjoyment of life and written this book to help you enjoy yours!

It's important to note that alongside my journey with Gratitude, I have made other positive changes in my life that have complemented it:

- Being a stalwart gatekeeper of the thoughts I allow space for in my mind
- Regular exercise
- Connecting with nature
- Shaking my caffeine addiction and reducing alcohol intake

I would liken my relationship with Gratitude as a wise and kind friend holding my hand through the day, or a guardian angel watching over my energy!

How about you?

I hope you've enjoyed taking this journey together, please be kind to yourselves on this journey - remember, Kindness and Gratitude are beloved siblings!

Pool of Practices

This chapter contains a selection of activities, games and practices to help you bring Gratitude to life in mindful, meaningful and fun ways. You can think of this chapter as a foundation for your Gratitude toolkit, a space where you add any nourishing exercises to grow your own personal pool, that you can dip into or even bathe in when you want to nourish your wellbeing, nurture your spiritual journey or cultivate more positive experiences.

Recording your Practices and Learning

In order to cement and build on your learning, I invite you to choose the most nourishing ways to record anything that arises for you from the practices – vision boards or collages, post it notes, calendar reminders, jingles, dances, poems, whatever feels fun and helps you embed your learning! Here are some ideas:

- Positive Post It Notes - jot down your learning/gratitude on notelets or Post It Notes and find somewhere meaningful to display them.

- Gratitude Jar - write them down on notes and put them inside a jar that you can decorate as you wish.

- Gratitude Tree - make a small tree from foraged twigs, cut out some paper shapes in the style of your choosing (e.g leaves, hearts etc.), write your golden reflections on them and attach them to the tree with string or ribbon.

- Gratitude Board - as with Positive Post Its, put up a Gratitude Board somewhere you can see it every day, and add what you're grateful for as often as you wish. Notice how you feel when doing the practice of:
    - Thinking of something you're grateful for
    - Gratitude naturally arising and you feeling called to add it to your board
    - Placing a gratitude note on your board
    - Seeing the board fill up with notes.
- Gratitude Journal - note down the silver linings or golden reflections that you become aware of in the Gratitude Journal at the back of this book, or get yourself a separate one. Do this as frequently as you wish.

You can also use song, poetry, dance, sculpture, photography, film or any other method of self-expression for this - choose whatever feels good.

The Honour Roll

You can do this in any way that speaks to your own individuality, feelings beliefs or brain type, but here are a few suggestions:

Logical List

Working backwards from, for example, the food on your plate, and asking yourself:

What makes it possible for me to be eating this food?

Mindful Mind Map

Take a piece of paper and write or draw the meal you've had in the middle. Let your mind wander and explore all the parts of the process that resulted in your food ending up in front of you. Add as many categories as you like, and ask some mindful questions such as:

People – Who was involved? E.g. Me, people who put the food on the supermarket shelf, people who delivered it to the store, people who packaged it, people who picked the ingredients.

Mother Earth/Nature – How did the earth provide this food?

Equipment – How did I come to be sitting on this furniture, eating with these utensils?

Physical/Actions – How am I able to sit and eat here?

Gratitude A to Z

Stick a sheet of paper on your fridge with the alphabet on it. When you go to the fridge, see if you can fill in something you're grateful for beginning with a letter of the alphabet. You can make it more of a team activity by inviting others who live with you to join in, with each person using a chosen coloured pen. You can even make it a competition!

Gratitude Inventory

Literally take stock of everything within you, around you, and beyond, that is helping you in life, making things easier for you or enabling you to do things you would otherwise be unable to do. Start by what you can see, what is supporting you to read this book in this current moment.

Gratitude Hierarchy

Take a look at the model of Maslow's Hierarchy of Needs in Chapter 1 and try working your way up to see how your needs are being met. Try these mindful questions, remembering not to judge yourself if difficult emotions arise.

Do you have the freedom and ability to breathe?

Do you feel reasonably healthy?

Do you have food and drink and even the ability to choose them?

Do you have a working fridge that keeps everything fresh and prevents it from going to waste or making you ill?

Do you have a place to shelter that is warm in winter?

Do you have soft furnishings to decorate the space with colour and for added comfort?

Do you have enough hot and cold running water to keep yourself and your space clean?

If you'd like to develop this practice, think of some other questions that help you explore the ways your needs are being met on each level.

Layered Meditation

When I first started meditating, I found it really difficult to 'stop thinking', until I realised that stopping thinking was counterproductive! I tried layering my meditation, allowing myself the kindness of a mental run up, so to speak, before floating into the stillness or intention I had set. I found that by doing two minutes where I provide a positive focus to occupy my mind in a direction that is nourishing and soothing, after the two minutes my mind is already calmer, and I can then either go straight into the meditation or take another two minutes of mindfulness (for example following my breath as it flows in and out of my body or simply noticing my thoughts) and then finally either just letting go with a still mind, or meditating on the intention I have set myself.

My golden rule with meditation is, it's your way or the highway! Meditation is about connecting with your inner self, and this is absolutely unique, so don't worry about how, when, where and how long other people do it for – have fun experimenting and find the ways that are most nourishing for you. Layered meditations have become my go to, but they may not satisfy everyone's needs and preferences. If you're not confident when it comes to meditating, have the self-kindness to set yourself small easy goals, for example, start with 10-30 seconds of listing what you're grateful for, just let the thoughts roll, and you may find it difficult to think of things (not by the end of this book though!), or you might find yourself in a positive spiral, where your list continues to flow, or tangents into different areas. As you practise and feel like it's working, you may want to give yourself more time, and find that the benefits increase – perhaps you feel even calmer, perhaps you get some inspired ideas, perhaps you feel a deeper connection with your inner self, or something else!

Resources:

- Insight Timer App or any app that allows you to set multiple bells – it's a good idea to set this up in advance and have the app open and ready, as it can be fiddly and cause a distraction! (If you're not able to use the app, set a timer for 1 minute and simply reset it when it goes off.)

- A safe, comfortable space to meditate

- A set amount of time where you will not be interrupted and can focus only on yourself, even for a short while

- An intention of what you'd like to get out of the time – when you feel you're calm and present enough in your quiet space, take a moment to ask yourself what you need most right now. Try to let it be simple, give yourself the gift of not overthinking and allow it to be whatever feels easiest (some examples: to feel peaceful, to nourish myself, to relax for a few minutes)

Guidance:

1) Get yourself into a comfortable position, whatever that means for you

2) Take a few breaths at your own pace and depth to bring yourself into the present moment as best you can

3) When you feel you're calm and present enough, ask yourself what you'd like to get out of this meditation – try not to keep it simple, give yourself the gift of not overthinking and allow it to whatever feels easiest (some examples, to feel peaceful, to nourish myself, to relax for a few minutes)

4) Repeat your intention, in your mind or out loud, 3 times to help you settle into it and accept it as the focus of your energy during this time

5) Decide what 'shape' your meditation will take – e.g 1 minute of Gratitude, followed by 1 minute of mindfulness, followed by 1 minute of relaxing – remember it's good to play around and see what works – 3 layers may be too much, but the purpose of the layering is to ease yourself into a relaxing mind space.

Self-Care Check In

- Find a quiet place if possible

- Take a few breaths to bring your awareness into your body

- Notice any thoughts that may be present and wave hello to them (that way you're not judging, just mindfully noticing)

- Start a body scan from the top of your hair to the tips of your toenails, tuning in to see if there is anything that doesn't feel comfortable, right or pleasant (tension, pain, hunger, tiredness, imbalance) - the intention is to offer yourself a measure of how you're feeling physically (this can be on a numerical scale, say 0 - 10 or in any other way that feels helpful, for example, adjectives, percentage, colours, weather etc.)

- As your awareness travels through the whole of your body, if you notice anything that feels uncomfortable, take a point away from 10 - if it's low level, maybe half a point, and if it's stronger maybe 2 points.

- When you've reached the end, notice with kindness what score or result you have

- Then, if you need to, ask yourself, "What can I do to move myself up the scale by 1 point?" (if you're not using numerical values, try "What can I do to help myself feel a little better?") - remember to keep yourself safe and encourage yourself to make healthy choices as much as possible. If you're unsure about what's healthy for you, please seek advice from a trusted health professional.

References

1) Alidina, S (2015), It's Not Mindfulness Without Kindness. Available at: https://www.mindful.org/its-not-mindfulness-without-kindness/ Accessed 10th July 2024

2) Maslow, A (1943) A Theory of Human Motivation, Psychological Review, American Psychological Association

3) McLeod, S (January 2024), Maslow's Hierarchy of Needs. Available at: https://www.simplypsychology.org/maslow.html Accessed 4th April 2024

4) Mind (August 2023), How To Improve Your Mental Wellbeing. Available at: https://www.mind.org.uk/information-support/tips-for-everyday-living/wellbeing/ Accessed 10th July 2024

5) Des Marais, S (September 2022), Cognitive Signs of Stress. Available at: https://psychcentral.com/stress/the-impact-of-stress Accessed 12th July 2024

6) Olivine PhD MPH, A (March 2023), What Is the Sympathetic Nervous System? Available at:

https://www.verywellhealth.com/sympathetic-nervous-system-how-it-works-and-more-7107953
Accessed 12th July 2024

7) Rozin, P and Royzman, EB (November 2001), Negativity Bias, Negativity Dominance and Contagion, Personality and Social Psychology Review, 5(4), https://doi.org/10.1207/S15327957PSPR0504_2
Available at: https://journals.sagepub.com/doi/10.1207/S15327957PSPR0504_2
Accessed 22nd July 2024

8) Sha, Z G and Xiu, R (2017), Tao Science, The Science, Wisdom, and Practice of Creation and Grand Unification, Waterside Press

9) Unicef (July 2023), 'Drinking Water', 'Universal Access to Safe Drinking Water is a Fundamental Need and Human Right'. Available at:
https://data.unicef.org/topic/water-and-sanitation/drinking-water/
Accessed 29th July 2024

Thank you for reading Gratitude Goldmine.

Sarit would love to hear from you about your experiences with this book. You can connect with her via her website, www.highestgoodwellbeing.com, or on Instagram: @highestgoodwellbeing.

Printed in Great Britain
by Amazon